Joining Miracles

Navigating the Seas of Latent Possibility

To Bob Puglia,
In hopes that we all
slip into the perfect
Reality Track together.
Michael McGaulley
February, 2011

Companion book to the spiritual thriller,

The Grail Conspiracies

Michael McGaulley

Published in the United States of America by Champlain House Media. ChamplainHouseMedia. com.

This is a work of fiction. Any similarity to real persons or names, living or dead, or to actual events, organizations, or locales, is coincidental and not intended by the author.

This publication is designed to provide accurate and authoritative information with regard to the subject matter covered. It is sold with the understanding that the publisher and author are not engaged in rendering legal, accounting, or other professional advice. If legal advice or other expert assistance is required, the services of a competent professional persona should be sought.
> –Adapted from a Declaration of Principles jointly adopted by a Committee of the American Bar Association and a Committee of Publishers and Associations

The concepts and approaches attributed to the characters in this book, or by means of the references to the related book, *The Grail Conspiracies*, are based on the author's research, as well as on the author's imagination in extending existing theories in quantum physics, cosmology, human psychology and higher human potentials, and related fields, to the realm of what *might* be possible.

Library of Congress Cataloguing-in-Publication Data can be obtained from the publisher upon request.

ISBN-10: 0-9768406-1-8
ISBN-13: 978-0976840619

First Edition: 2007.
10 9 8 7 6 5 4 3 2 1

"What if you slept? And what if in your sleep, you dreamed? And what if in your dream you went to heaven and there plucked a strange and beautiful flower? And what if when you awoke, you had the flower in your hand? Ah! What then?"
                    Samuel Taylor Coleridge

"... the universe begins to look more like a great thought than a great machine."
                    Sir James Jeans

"We are not human beings having a spiritual experience. We are spiritual beings having a human experience."
                    Pierre Teilhard de Chardin, S.J.

"So the old word observer simply has to be crossed off the books, and we must put in the new word participator. In this way we've come to realize that the universe is a participatory universe."
                    John Archibald Wheeler

"There are only two ways to live your life. One is as though nothing is a miracle. The other is as though everything is. I believe in the latter."
                    Albert Einstein

1

REALITY
IS NOT AS IT SEEMS

1

Two Years Ago

MY FOOT SLIPPED ON THE WET ROCK; searing pain shot up from my ankle; the leg gave way; I toppled off the edge of the narrow trail into the emptiness below.

I can't say my whole life passed before my eyes then, just the two principles I'd been living by:

Whatever *can* go wrong, *will* go wrong—that's Murphy's Law.

And then there's my First Corollary to Murphy's Law: Once *one* thing goes wrong, *everything else* does, too.

I SUPPOSE I SOUND LIKE A GROUCH, A WHINER, A LOSER. The fact is, I *was* a loser back then, angry and frustrated, convinced that there was some sort of cosmic conspiracy to make my life even more difficult.

It seemed to be more than just coincidence that I lived constantly on the verge of getting the things I wanted, only to find them snatched away (as I had come to expect) at the last moment.

It seemed more than irony that the things I most dreaded and guarded *against* were precisely those that *did* come about, producing precisely what I most definitely *did not* want.

It seemed that every time something could go one way or the other, it invariably went the worst way—from the toast falling jelly-side down, to traffic lights ganging up on me when I was in a rush, to the really big, bad things in life.

"Bad luck," if you want to call it that, seemed to come along for me much more often than random chance would indicate. And I was tired of it.

THEY SAY THAT YOU HAVE TO HIT BOTTOM before you can start heading up. In my case, that was literally true: you can't hit bottom much harder than when you fall off a mountain, as I did. At that point, you can either give up, or start climbing.

My tumble off a mountain trail in a driving, cold rainstorm, seemed to be more of the usual bad luck I had come to expect.

Ironically, however, it turned out to be the best thing that ever happened to me.

The fall showed me that I *had* been right: bad luck *did* come my way more often than mere chance. But not because I was the victim of a cosmic conspiracy to make my life difficult.

The fact is, I had been *choosing to* have those bad things happen to me. (Sounds strange, I suppose, but I'll explain later.)

In short, I learned that while there was no cosmic conspiracy out to get me, there is a set of "cosmic rules" governing the workings of our world. These rules can work *for* us or *against* us . . . and I was, without realizing it, choosing to have them work against me!

Most importantly, with the help of a strange old monk, I began to understand and apply these rules ("The Knowledge," as he called it) in navigating my life, so that now I'm on-course toward the outcomes I really want.

Now what *seem* to be "coincidences" almost invariably fall my way.

Which is how I ended up writing this little book.

2

THE FIRST THING TO GO WRONG—the event that I was convinced set off that cycle of "everything" seeming to go wrong—was losing my job a couple of weeks before the wedding.

Rather, before the *planned* wedding. Jackie felt we had no choice: "It would be imprudent without the security of two incomes."

Jackie, even more than I, was ever on the lookout for the risks and dangers in life. Looking back, I wonder if that shared fear was our greatest bond.

I had already paid the deposit—half the total cost of the whole trip. Hiking in Europe was something I'd dreamed about for years. I thought it over for most of one sleepless night, then decided that I was already so far in that it made no sense to walk away from that deposit . . . especially since it wasn't likely I'd ever get another chance to go, given my luck and my career prospects.

"I can't believe it," Jackie responded. "I can't believe I came so close to marrying someone as irresponsible as you're turning out to be."

Since then, it had just been one of those months.

MY SECOND COROLLARY TO MURPHY'S LAW: There's nothing so bad it can't get worse, and probably will . . . sooner rather than later.

Things did get worse, of course . . . just as I expected. It came as no surprise when the plane had mechanical problems along the way. I had nothing else to do in that cold, dreary terminal than sit and wonder, What comes next? Will my luggage turn up missing? Will I miss the train? Will the hotel lose my reservation?

The answer was predictable: all of the above.

Though I was slightly wrong on the details. The hotel didn't actually *lose* my reservation; instead they *gave* it away. "You were due hours ago," the desk clerk said when I finally arrived tired, grungy, and wet from a drenching rain.

"There was trouble with the plane. Then I found out that my luggage didn't arrive, and that caused me to miss the express train."

"You should have telephoned."

"I couldn't find a phone that worked." (Another Basic Rule of Life, as I saw things then: There's never a phone when you need one.)

"Alas, the room has now gone to someone else, not ten minutes ago."

"But my reservation—I've already paid for the room."

The clerk shrugged. "I know nothing of that. Perhaps you paid the travel agent, not the hotel."

"But—"

"There is another room I can let you have."

"Fine. I'll take it."

"But it can be for one night only."

"One night? But my reservation is for a week."

"That room, alas, has gone to someone else for this week." She smiled. "However, it is always possible that there will be a cancellation in the morning."

BUT IN THE MORNING THERE WAS STILL NO ROOM FOR ME. "Perhaps later something will turn up," the proprietor said. "Spend a few hours walking in the mountains, and luck may be with you."

Luck *is* with me: I already knew that. But it's *bad* luck, always bad luck.

"All my hiking gear was in my suitcase, and the airline lost it."

"The hotel will be happy to store your bag for you when it arrives. The trails are gentle here. You won't need equipment."

"What if it rains?"

"Why expect the worst?"

3

I SET OFF ON A PERFECT MORNING, just warm enough to be ideal for hiking, with not a cloud in the sky.

Enjoy it while you've got it, I told myself: a day like this is too good to last.

The trail began with an easy stroll across soft green pastures still damp with morning dew, then rose through a pine forest, heavy with the scent of balsam and wildflowers.

After an hour, I came to the first lookout. From up here, the village looked like a collection of toy houses. The mountains, snow-capped and majestic, soared above the valley.

Mountains have always been magical places for me. Up there in the clear air and brilliant sunshine, I began to break out of the dark mood that had been hanging over me for weeks—the sense of defeat, the mindset that I was a helpless victim of events conspiring against me. Up there, I was annoyed at myself for the time I'd wasted wallowing in self-pity.

Maybe, just maybe, things will work out, I told myself. Maybe my luck will turn. Maybe a room will turn up. Maybe the airline will get my bag to me. Maybe I'll have clean clothes tonight.

Maybe even a decent job will turn up when I get home.

Things had been going badly for me, no doubt about it, but that's life. Into each life some rain must fall, and so forth.

As the word "rain" came into my thoughts, I looked up and noticed the first clouds drifting over the tops of the mountains.

The early drops hit as I came to the signpost for the alternate route back to the village: the worst possible time, when I was at the farthest point from shelter. My usual luck.

The initial drizzle escalated into a downpour. Mist developed, blocking the view of the valley. I lost my sense of direction as I raced back down the trail, hoping I was still headed toward the village.

In my rush, I missed the marker for the main trail.

Which is why I was racing across slippery wet rocks, and how, some time later, I woke up to find myself lying on a rocky ledge, my clothes soaked through, rain beating on my back.

I tried to stand. Pain shot up my leg, and I dropped back onto the rock. My head throbbed, and I felt a lump on my forehead. I checked my watch, to see how long I had been out. It had stopped when I fell, and now it blinked 12:00, 12:00, 12:00.

Once one thing goes wrong, everything goes wrong.

NOW I'VE REALLY DONE IT, I thought. Lost on a mountain with a broken ankle, my only set of clothes soaked through, and almost certainly no room waiting for me even if I could make it back down to the village.

The wind began to pick up, and now I spotted the first snowflakes. I was becoming more and more chilled, and knew I was going to come out of this with the worst cold of my life. Maybe even pneumonia. Just what I needed.

Once one thing goes wrong—I was used to that scenario. But this time it wasn't just events conspiring to make my life difficult: This time it was literally life-and-death. Soaked through by a cold rain, hobbled with a broken ankle, I was in major trouble. The possibilities ran through my head: Hypothermia, exposure, frostbite, death. Not a pleasant menu.

Since I was no longer registered at a hotel in the village, no one would notice if I failed to return from the mountain. Even worse, I wasn't just lost on the trail, I was trapped on a ledge below the trail. It could be too late by the time anyone spotted me.

I sat there in the rain, cold and frightened. What had I done to deserve this? Why couldn't things ever go right for me?

That's when I spotted the little footpath that twisted down from the rock ledge. I broke off a branch of a tree to use as a makeshift cane, pulled myself to my feet, and hobbled down the trail.

The trail wound its way back into the forest, and before long I came upon a little chapel, nearly overgrown by trees. It looked abandoned, but at least it would provide shelter from the rain and cold.

Then I caught myself: Don't get your hopes up. The way things are going, the door will probably be locked.

I tried the handle. To my surprise, the door opened. I stepped inside.

4

IT WAS SNUG AND DRY INSIDE THE CHAPEL, and the windows still held stained glass. At least I was out of the wind and rain.

I dropped into one of the old wooden pews. It felt good to sit. I was soaked to the skin; I'd soon be chilled now that I'd stopped moving.

But with a broken ankle, I couldn't keep moving.

I thought I'd hit bottom out on the trail. Now I found that had been just a resting point on the way down to the real pit of despair. Everything I'd worked for was slipping away. The job I had put so much into—gone. Jackie and the wedding and that future—gone. The money I'd saved for this trip—wasted.

Even if—best case—I did somehow manage to make it back to the village, I'd be spending the rest of my stay in a hospital, locked into a leg cast. Between medical bills and the extra cost of getting home with a cast on the leg, I'd be up to my neck in debt—and have nothing to show for it.

I was cold and tired and depressed, and for that moment, I really didn't want to go on. Once one thing goes wrong— well, that opens the way for everything else to dump on you. I was tired of it all. Tired even of living.

THEN I NOTICED CARVINGS ON ONE OF THE STONE WALLS.

I pulled myself to my feet and hobbled over to get a closer look. I couldn't read the words, but that was no surprise: this was a foreign country.

What did surprise me was that I didn't even recognize the alphabet used in the inscription. It wasn't ours, and it wasn't Hebrew or Russian or Arabic or even ancient Egyptian.

Then what language was it? Or was it in code?

I saw movement out of the corner of my eye. A figure materialized from the shadows. I was suddenly frightened, realizing how vulnerable I was with this bad leg. Running was out of the question, and so was fighting.

But it turned out to be only a small old man. His face was kindly, and his eyes twinkled with—was it joy or amusement? His bald head was round and shiny, and a fringe of snowy white hair circled around behind his ears, then looped down to a white beard. He wore a plain brown woolen robe. A monk's robe, I realized, and it was old and patched.

He smiled and held out his hand. "Peace, my friend. There is no reason for fear."

I relaxed. He seemed safe enough. I introduced myself, and took his hand. It was rough, strong for such a small old man.

"I am Brother Freddie, the Keeper of the Knowledge."

"I didn't mean to intrude. I was lost. I thought the chapel was abandoned. I didn't—"

" Of course you were lost. The Knowledge drew you."

I didn't know if he meant it as a question or a statement. "The knowledge? You mean that inscription? It seems very old."

"They say it is even older than the chapel."

"How old is that?"

He shook his head and smiled. "No one knows. This was a holy place, a power spot, long before the chapel was built."

"I can't read the carvings."

He smiled. "It would take an unusual visitor to read them. They are written in a very old language."

I waited, expecting him to translate. But he was silent. From the expression in his eyes, I knew he was assessing me.

"You have found your way to the Knowledge," he said. Again, something in the way he said the word told me that, in his view, this was Knowledge with a capital K.

Why this bizarre conversation? I asked myself. Why are we standing here talking? I'm lost, I'm wet, I'm chilled through, I have a broken ankle, and maybe a concussion. I need to get back to the village, not discuss some old carvings on a wall.

"I'm not sure—" I started to say, then stopped.

"You have found your way here because you needed to be here."

"That's true enough. In this weather, I wouldn't survive outside."

He smiled and shook his head. "No, you found your way here not just for today, not just to escape the rain."

I couldn't help myself. I laughed despite the pain in my head and leg, laughed even though I was shivering from the wet and cold. I laughed because I was on the verge of panic.

"Sorry," I said after I settled down. "I know I shouldn't be laughing in a chapel, but it just seems so ludicrous. I definitely did not 'find' my way here. I'm here because I'm totally lost."

"Yes, of course," the Old Monk said. "Yes, that's the way it usually is. People find their way to the Knowledge when they are most totally lost."

I wanted to get warm and dry and safe, not get drawn into a conversation about some carvings on a rock. Kindly as he seemed, this old monk could turn out to be a fanatic. If I let him get started, would he ever stop?

"The Knowledge? Are you referring to those carvings on the wall?"

"Those inscriptions convey the core of the Knowledge."

"But what is the Knowledge?"

He peered closely at me, and I felt he was somehow looking through me. Then he said, "The Knowledge enables one to—"

He cut himself off and shook his head. "No, I'll not say more. Not now. Not until . . . not until you're certain you want to know more."

"No? Why not?"

"Because if you once absorb and learn to live by the Knowledge, then your life will change. Forever."

5

MY ANKLE WAS TOO PAINFUL TO STAND ON. I slumped back into a wooden pew. "You mean simply by knowing what this inscription says, I'd be changed forever?"

"If you absorb the Knowledge, if you make it fully a part of how you view the world and how you live in it, if you live as the Knowledge teaches, then, yes, your life will change forever: You will live better and happier and more productively."

Obviously, he was a fanatic, a zealot, and I should get away from him while I could, before he really got rolling.

But with this ankle, in this weather, getting away was impossible. It would be suicidal to start down the mountain in a storm like this. I was his captive audience.

Besides, curiosity drew me on. "Change my life? These carvings? How?"

"The Knowledge provides a way of taking active control of the events and circumstances you encounter in life."

My face must have shown that I didn't understand. He went on: "In other words, the Knowledge provides a methodology for joining the Reality Tracks that lead to beneficial outcomes."

I felt my head spin. "Methodology? Reality Tracks? Beneficial Outcomes?" In a sentence, it seemed we'd jumped from the medieval to the world of high-tech. Was he a Harvard M.B.A. disguised as a 12th Century monk?

"Are you telling me that this Knowledge provides a sure way of getting what I want?"

"A sure way?" He shook his head. "Oh no, not sure, not sure at all. After all, quantum physics tells us there is no certainty, only probability, in this material world. Indeed, there is, so they tell us, only a probability that the atoms that comprise these stone walls stay in their anticipated orbits and hold the walls together."

I glanced up, I suppose expecting to see the stones dissolve. It had been that kind of month.

He chuckled and gently touched me on the arm. "Not to be alarmed, my young friend. It's only a way of looking at reality. The probabilities favor the stones remaining intact, just as the probabilities favor your strong expectations coming to be. The Knowledge provides a way of greatly increasing the probability of experiencing desired outcomes. Under the One, of course."

I wasn't much of a church-goer—my family never had been into that. But it was obvious what he meant by that part about 'under the One.'

I let it pass for the moment. "What do you mean by 'increasing the probability?'"

"Would you prefer the long or the short explanation?"

I WAS SURE THAT MY ANKLE WAS BROKEN. It seemed I could even hear the broken edges of the bone scraping together. My head throbbed. Maybe I'd gotten a concussion in the fall. My clothes were still soaked through, and my chest was tightening up: I was probably on the way to a monumental cold, more likely pneumonia. I needed to get warm and dry and safe, not discuss some inscriptions (that might or might not be ancient) with a strange old man (who might or might not be a real monk).

In the best of circumstances, with all limbs in perfect shape, it was a couple of hours' walk back down to the village. If I didn't make it down by dark in this weather, then I'd be in real trouble. But with a broken ankle, there was no way I could walk down the mountain.

"I'd like to talk about the inscriptions another time, but right now I think my ankle is broken. Is there a phone here? Any way to call down to the village for help?"

"Perhaps now is a good time for you to test the Knowledge, to learn how to apply it in your own life?"

"I need to get to a doctor. Soon," I said, and then I sneezed—a sneeze that welled up from deep inside me and echoed off the stone walls of the chapel.

Brother Freddie looked shocked. "Oh my, my, there I am with my head in the clouds again! Tsk, tsk, isn't that just like a monk? You're wet, you're cold, and I'm oblivious. And of course it is one of our missions here at the monastery to help travelers. Oh my, my, shame on me."

He jumped to his feet and hurried into a back room. He emerged with a couple of blankets. You can wrap up with these while I go over to the main building for a few minutes. We'll see what we can do about your ankle."

"Thank you. You're very kind."

"Ah, but I am a monk. Kindness is my job."

6

BROTHER FREDDIE RETURNED, pushing an antique wooden wheelchair. I managed to pull myself into it without re-injuring my ankle, and he wheeled me out of the chapel and along a covered arcade to another old stone building all but invisible behind a cluster of pines.

This, I realized, was the main building of an old monastery. I'd failed to see it when I arrived because of the trees that had overgrown the area. It seemed huge for one old monk, but of course it had been built at a time when monks were more plentiful than today.

As we went along the arcade, I felt how sharply the temperature had dropped. The rain was mixing now with snow and sleet, and it hissed as it hit the ground in the monastery courtyard.

I'd never been in a monastery before, for that matter don't think I'd ever seen a monk. Now I found myself trapped with a monk—a mad monk?—in a monastery. On a mountain. In a storm. Helpless with a broken ankle.

We entered through the kitchen, and it smelled of apples and baking bread and soups and spices. He pushed through a door, and we headed down a long corridor.

It was more austere inside than I expected. Simple wooden furniture, walls bare except for a cross here and there, and some other religious symbols I didn't recognize.

Finally, as he pushed open a heavy wooden door, I found myself in a library, lined floor to ceiling with thousands of old, leather-bound books. A fire crackled in the fireplace, and I saw a few soft chairs scattered around. A big television set hooked to a video-recorder filled most of one corner of the room.

My head snapped back in a double-take. A color TV and VCR up here in the mountains? I wouldn't have expected to find electricity here, let alone this kind of electronic gadgetry. I was under the impression that monks spent their time copying manuscripts, not watching TV.

Am I hallucinating? I wondered. Maybe I'm still lying out there in the rain on that cliff, freezing to death, dreaming all this.

He guided me to one of the chairs, a soft recliner. That, at least, was no hallucination, and I shifted from the wheelchair to sink into its comforting soft warmth.

He shuffled back the way he had come, and returned with a towel, an old woolen sweater, and a pair of dry pants. All were patched and worn, but freshly laundered. The clothing seemed to be about my size.

He left again, and I pulled off my wet clothes. I dried with the towel, and pulled on the sweater. Somehow I managed to slide my wet trousers off and the dry ones on without causing damage to the injured ankle. It was too painful to think of removing the shoe, but the heat from the fire radiated through the leather and warmed the foot.

I'D BEEN DOZING WHEN I looked up and saw him holding a tray. He pulled a rough-hewn oak table around in front of my chair, then set the table, placing a big bowl of steaming soup for each of us, along with a loaf of crusty bread.

He settled across from me in an old wooden chair, then spread his hands over the food, and his lips moved in a quiet prayer. I realized for the first time just how hungry I was.

He broke some of his bread and dropped it into the soup, so I did the same. It was a hearty mix of vegetables, rice, beans, and spices, and the bread was coarse and filling. The perfect meal for a damp, chilly day in the mountains.

I tried a sip of the red wine he poured from an earthen jug. It was a local wine, nothing subtle about it, but it was warming and pleasant.

We ate in silence for a couple of minutes. He seemed as hungry as I. I couldn't help thinking what a peculiar but lovable old man he was.

I WAS BEGINNING TO FEEL A LITTLE BETTER. But I couldn't forget that I still had a broken ankle, and that I was still a long way up a mountainside—in a snowstorm.

"I appreciate all that you've done for me, Brother Freddie. You saved my life, the lunch was wonderful. But now I do need to get to a doctor."

"You speak of a broken ankle. Is that truly the track in reality you want?"

"Track in reality? I don't know what you mean"

"Do you really want to spend the next weeks hobbled by a broken ankle?"

"Do I want a broken ankle? Of course not. But that's the way it is."

"The way it is in one Reality Track, that's true. But you are free to join a different Reality Track, if you choose."

"Join a different track? My ankle is broken: what other tracks are there? A broken ankle isn't something I can choose to have or not have."

"What other tracks are there?, you ask. Our friends who work in the strange field of quantum physics tell us there are an *infinity* of tracks. And in certain of those tracks, you would find that your ankle is perfectly healthy. Would you not prefer to join one of those happier tracks?"

"Join a track? Like I'd step from one train onto another?" I blurted. I needed a doctor, not just word games.

"Your difficulty, my young friend, stems from the fact that you accept the reality that *seems* to be before you as the *only possible* reality. Once you understand that what we assume to be reality is actually a construction of our minds, then all possibilities open."

7

"WHAT WE ACCEPT AS REALITY IS ACTUALLY A CONSTRUCTION OF OUR MINDS?" I couldn't have heard that right. "I really do need to get to a doctor."

He picked up the television's remote control and pushed a couple of buttons. The screen flared to life.

"What do you see?"

"A soccer match."

"True, on one level you do see soccer. But what do you actually see?"

That puzzled me for a moment, then I understood. You mean beyond the picture? "I see a television screen. I see colors."

"The fact is, you see a mirage."

"A mirage?"

"Exactly. What you actually see is nothing more than tiny dots of light—or 'pixels,' as the tech people call them—flashing on and off. The pixels create the sense of color and movement. Our minds have learned to translate those moving colors into what we accept as the representation of a soccer match in progress."

"Well, in that sense, sure. What's on the TV is a mirage, that's true. But of course it's obvious that what's on the TV screen is not *actual* reality, just a broadcast."

He smiled and shook his head. "In fact, there is less difference than you might think. Our eyes pick up certain energy waves from the television screen, and our brains translate those signals into a sense of reality—that is, informing us that the moving lights on the screen represent people and soccer balls. In much the same way, our eyes pick up energy waves reflected from things that are actually around us, not just on a screen, and our brains translate those signals into a similar sense of reality."

"But there's a big difference." I pointed to the battered old table between us. "What's on the TV screen is just light images, but this table is real. I'm really seeing this table in the real world, not just the television world. Television gives us *virtual* reality, not actual reality."

"Then shall we talk about, as you call it, 'actual' reality? This table, for instance. What do you actually see?"

"I see an old wooden table."

He shook his head. "No, you do not see a table."

"It sure looks like a table to me."

"Ah, but that is the illusion created by your senses and your brain working together. What you 'see' is the effect of your brain translating some coded electromagnetic signals into what we have designated as 'table.'"

"I'm over my head."

"We think we see the color and height of a table—or of a rose or a sunset or a mountain, or even a face. But our 'seeing' is all internal, within ourselves. In the world outside our brains, there is no such thing as color, there is not even such a thing as solidity. There are, in the external world, only energy and electromagnetic waves of varying types, which our brains, acting with our senses, convert into the perception of color and shape and solidity. The eyes pick up these light waves, and the brain translates the signals to 'table,' or 'mountain' or whatever."

I nodded, remembering something like this from my school-days. Useless academic stuff, I'd figured—stuff I'd memorized and then forgotten.

"The first point is this: We don't perceive what is *really* there, but rather what we *believe should be* there. Our minds construct the sense of solid reality from what are in actuality only faint waves of energy. Our minds construct that sense of solidity because nothing in this physical world is as it seems."

He tapped that table—illusionary though it may be—to emphasize the words he repeated. "What we experience as 'reality' in this physical world is not as it seems."

8

"NOTHING IN THE PHYSICAL WORLD IS AS IT SEEMS? Maybe so, but I've functioned well enough through life oblivious of that fact."

"Aren't you concerned that perhaps you're missing the real point?"

"Real point of what?"

"Is this table solid?" he asked, again pointing to the battered wooden table on which we had eaten our lunch. It looked as though it had been there since time immemorial.

I knocked on the wood. "Is it solid? It's as solid as they come. They don't make them like this any more."

He laughed. "But it's not solid, it only appears to be solid. The wood is comprised of atoms, which are 99.99% empty space. The solid appearance is an illusion."

He paused for me to absorb that, then added, "Now reach over and give it another good knock."

I knocked on it so hard my knuckles stung.

"This is where it becomes really interesting. Your hand is also made up of atoms, hence is in fact no more solid than the table. Your hand, like the atoms that comprise it, is 99.99% empty space."

He paused, then added, "Granted, that concept may be difficult to grasp, but it is nonetheless true."

I nodded, though I wasn't sure that I saw his point.

He said, "You look at the table and see solid wood. A physicist would look at the same table and see mostly empty space."

"But if it's just empty space, then why does it look and feel solid? How can I touch it or knock on it and get the sense of solidity?"

He chuckled. "Good questions. Questions that science is still puzzling over. By one theory, it's because the electrons within the atom spin incredibly fast around the nucleus, and that spin creates the sense of solidity. The table stays together because the atoms follow certain laws of probability, tending to stay in predictable orbits."

"I'M NOT CLEAR WHERE THIS IS GOING."

"The point is this: we are too inclined to believe what our eyes and other senses are telling us. Your eyes tell you it's a table—or they tell you it's a building you're looking at. Or your ears tell you it's the barking of a dog, or the roar of a jet. You accept the table or the jet or the mountain as the reality, and never look through to the more profound reality that beyond the appearance there is *not* a table, not a jet, *only energy waves* emanating."

I was silent.

"As I said earlier, we move through life conditioned to believe what our eyes and ears tell us is 'reality.' But actual reality is quite different."

"Different in what way?"

"We live not in a universe of solid things, but rather in a universe of energy. Energy and mass, as Einstein pointed out, are ultimately interchangeable."

"I'm afraid I'm missing your point."

"It's the point I made earlier: nothing is as it seems. Reality, as we know it, is largely a construction of our minds. The discoveries of modern science are confirming the intuitive insights of the ancient wisdom—as expressed, for instance, in the Knowledge. Putting it differently, the Knowledge, along with the teachings and actions of the ancients, provided an intuitive prefiguring of many of the findings that modern scientists are now confirming."

"'Intuitive prefiguring?'"

"As you know, there are numerous accounts, not only in the Bible but in other literature as well, of the seemingly inexplicable, mysterious, even almost magical events and outcomes produced by people celebrated as mystics and saints. Those mystics didn't offer an explanation for how they did what they did, they just proceeded to cure, to bring about unexpected events and outcomes, to do what seemed impossible. Beyond that, many of them insisted that they were not unique beings, but rather role models that others could emulate.

"Many people, maybe most people, have rejected the stories of miraculous events as 'mere legends,' 'fairy-tales,' 'nice stories,' and even lies because they violated the laws of causality. But St. Augustine, himself intuitively prefiguring the knowledge yet to be discovered, wrote, 'miracles happen, not in opposition to nature but in opposition to what we know of nature.'

"Now, as the tools of modern science open up fresh insights into the true nature of reality, and what is possible within that larger reality, we're beginning to realize that these seeming miracles were not in opposition to nature, but rather consistent with the potentials implicit within nature all along.

"The mystics may not have had access to today's scientific vocabulary, but they knew—intuitively—what was possible, and acted accordingly to show the rest of us what we could do."

"Oh?"

"The findings of modern science and modern thinkers help us understand how physical reality—that is, reality as we think we know it—is largely a construction of our minds. Today's technology demonstrates that we live in a flexible world that is mostly energy."

He paused, then added, "And once we grasp the implications that flow from that—that the world in which we live is largely energy, and that our minds are also forms of energy—then a totally different view of reality opens up."

"Why are you telling me this?"

"To prepare you for the Knowledge."

"By shaking my faith in reality?" I said, only partially in jest.

"Exactly so."

I   REALITY IS NOT AS IT SEEMS

❏   The Knowledge provides a methodology for joining the Reality Tracks that lead to beneficial outcomes.

❏   There are, in the external world, only energy and electromagnetic waves of varying types, which our brains, acting with our senses, convert into the perception of color and shape and solidity. The eyes pick up these light waves, and the brain translates the signals into 'table,' or 'mountain,' or whatever we term them.

❏   That is, we don't perceive what is *really* there, but rather what we *believe should be* there. Our minds construct the sense of solid reality from what are in actuality only these faint waves of energy.

❏   Thus, reality, as we know it, is largely a construction of our minds.

❏   Once we grasp the implications that flow from that—that the world in which we live is largely energy, and that our minds are also forms of energy, and hence that reality, as we know it, is largely a construction of our minds—then a totally different view of a deeper reality opens up.

II

ALL POTENTIAL REALITIES ALREADY EXIST

9

"THE ULTIMATE REALITY IS THAT I NEED TO GET off this mountain and to a hospital," I said. Enough of old inscriptions, enough of quantum physics and tables that aren't really solid. What was real was that my ankle was really hurting, and if I didn't get to a doctor soon I was going to be in even worse trouble.

"Why?"

"Because I've broken my ankle. It needs to be set before I do more damage."

"Bone, of course, is also 99.99% empty space. In a sense, it's hardly more solid than what we see on the television screen." He took the remote back and flicked to another channel, and then another.

"I need to—"

"We're totally unaware of the fact that even as we sit in this room a variety of alternate television channels are, in some strange way, right here with us."

He flicked the remote, then flicked again, and snippets of weather, news, a soap opera, and the soccer match again flashed across the screen. "We don't feel those other channels, we can't taste them or see or smell them. But they're real, nonetheless, latent windows on a virtual reality, waiting for us to join them."

"It's very urgent—"

"It's the same with computers," he said, pulling back a curtain to reveal a good-sized desktop. He moved the mouse, and the screen flared to life. "With a television, we change channels. With a computer, we call it hyper-linking. So it is that from one screen, with just the click of a mouse, we can hyper-link to another screen, opening up another whole new world of information. We can join that alternate link as easily as moving a finger."

To make his point, he hyper-linked from the news story on the screen to a background article on that topic, and from there to another bit of deeper background on another topic.

How about hyper-linking to something on how to care for a broken ankle? I wanted to say. Or how to survive a storm on a mountain despite an obsessed old monk.

"I really need to—"

"There are many alternate television channels available for us to join. You do see the analogy, don't you?"

"Analogy to what?"

"To the Knowledge, of course. Just as we can join another television channel by touching the right button on a remote, just as we can join another realm of data on the internet by clicking a mouse, so also the Knowledge enables us to elect to join other tracks in the physical reality we experience."

"JOIN OTHER TRACKS IN PHYSICAL REALITY? *How*? For that matter, *why*? And, by the way, what *is* a 'track in reality,' anyway?"

"You say you have injured your ankle?"

At last we were getting back to reality. "It's broken, I'm sure it's broken."

"Suppose it's not broken?"

"But it *is* broken, there's no changing that reality."

"Reality, keep in mind, is a construction of our minds, nothing more. With the guidance of the Knowledge, we have the ability to join more favorable courses in the reality we experience."

"What are you telling me?"

"Suppose you could step into a Reality Track in which your ankle is perfectly healthy? Suppose you could do that almost as easily as you change television channels?"

"Too bad things don't work that way. I need a doctor."

"Things don't work that way? How do you know that? Have you ever really tested the limits of the possible?"

"How would I do that—test the limits of the possible?" I asked to humor him while I figured out some way to get him to pay attention to the fact that my ankle was broken and that I desperately needed medical treatment.

"By applying the Knowledge."

"The Knowledge—the messages carved into that old stone wall? How can—"

"The Knowledge teaches us how to use the powers of the mind to shape the way in which the reality that we experience emerges from the sea of undifferentiated possibilities."

"The sea of what?"

"Our friends who work in the field of quantum physics tell us that until we enter the scene as observers — that is, as we experience it, or measure it, or observe it—all possible outcomes exist in an 'undifferentiated' state."

"'Undifferentiated? I'm not sure I know what that means."

"It's a state in which all is still potential, nothing is settled. All possibilities are out there, waiting for us to settle on the one we experience. At that point, those undifferentiated or latent possibilities reduce to the one which we experience as 'actual.'"

"Quantum physics is not exactly my area of expertise. What's unsettled?"

"Everything, absolutely everything—until we enter the equation. The core of all physical reality is nothing more than a sea of latent possibilities."

10

"SEA OF LATENT POSSIBILITIES? I seem to be adrift on that sea."

"We go through life accepting as fact that this old oak table is solid. But now, only in barely the past century, have we learned that the seemingly solid wood is made up of atoms, and in those atoms are sub-atomic particles, which in fact are 99.99% empty space. This table, appearing solid as an oak, is an illusion: the reality is that it is more than 99% empty. Everything in our world is the same. Your hand is 99.99% empty space, as I am, as is the food we eat, and everything else on this earth. When we 'see' or 'touch,' the reality is that our minds are constructing a sense of solid reality from the mirage of energy signals that are passed on by our senses. What we take as our normal physical reality is in a sense an illusion—the ultimate reality is down at the quantum level."

"As I said, I've always been content enough with physical reality—illusion though it may be."

"We somehow construct a sense of solidity and definiteness from what is ultimately fuzzy—'fuzzy,' that is, at the level of sub-atomic reality, quantum reality."

"Why not just ignore that quantum level and carry on with what we know is real?"

"Because quantum reality is also *our* reality. Those sub-atomic particles—the protons, neutrons and others yet to be discovered—are the building blocks of the physical world we experience."

I couldn't help thinking that I've survived this far in life without paying a particle of attention to quantum reality.

Then another thought came along: I've *survived* this far in life, but maybe not done so as well, or as happily, as maybe I might have. Maybe it was time to think about living by different rules—the rules of quantum reality, as expressed in The Knowledge. I should probably hear him out.

"You look at the table and see solidity, while a quantum physicist would look at the same table and see mostly empty space. Which view is correct? Both are. But if you can learn to work in both levels of reality, then marvelous possibilities open up to you."

"It's a little too late in life for me to go back for a degree in quantum physics."

He shook his head again. "You don't need that, you don't really need to know how it works, any more than you need to know how a television works in order to use it."

"So I'm sitting here on a wispy chair that's really 99.99% empty space, talking to the mirage of a monk named Freddie?"

He laughed again, a booming roar that echoed off the walls—the walls that were also, in the eyes of a physicist, 99.99% not really there.

"WHAT WE'RE TALKING ABOUT is not really so very difficult," the mirage that I took to be Brother Freddie said. "We only make it seem difficult by expecting it to be so."

He picked up the television remote and hit the On button. "Navigating this sea of indeterminate possibilities is not so very different from selecting a TV program. Which channel shall we choose?"

I hadn't come to the mountains to watch television, but out of politeness I said, "Let's try channel 2."

It came up, showing a tennis match.

He muted the sound. "Where was that program before I turned it on?"

"Where *was* that TV program?" That was something I'd never thought about before. I pondered a moment, then said, "Out there somewhere, I suppose. Somewhere in the atmosphere."

"Was it real before I tuned it in?"

I had to think on that one. "In a sense, yes, it was real. But real only in a latent sense until you flicked to it."

"Until we joined that channel, you mean? So channel 2 and 4 and 6 and 8 and so forth were all 'out there' someplace we non-techies don't understand, just waiting for us to tune them in—or 'join' them?"

"JOINING A REALITY TRACK is not so different from changing to a different television program," Brother Freddie repeated. "The array of possible TV channels is out there somewhere in the universe. We select the one we care to watch, hit the button, and it appears on the screen, as if waiting for us."

But real life isn't television, I wanted to say.

"In our real lives, an infinite array of possible futures—alternate Reality Tracks—as you said of television programs, are 'out there somewhere,' as if waiting for us to join them, alternative scenarios for us to step into."

11

I FOUND IT VERY HARD to get my mind around the idea that this solid world in which we live is not really solid, but rather is 99.99% empty space, and that the sense of solidity by which we live is an illusion. Equally hard to accept is the concept that every possible scenario exists out there, somewhere in the void, leading to every possible outcome.

Hardest of all to accept was what Brother Freddie was telling me—telling me, that is, courtesy of The Knowledge: That by holding a clear, focused intention I could shift from one scenario into another. What I *expected* played a key role in how reality *unfolded.*

"It seems very bizarre," I said.

"Bizarre, no question about that, but nonetheless consistent with the 'Many-Worlds' approach of Everett and Wheeler. That's the most widely accepted model now among those working in the field. You may be familiar with it?"

He paused for an instant, just long enough to be polite, not long enough to put me on the spot. Then he went on.

"The 'Many Worlds Hypothesis' suggests that perhaps all possible outcomes of an action exist, each in its own parallel reality." He shook his head. "Mind you, that's an extreme simplification, but it does give you the flavor of the concept."

"Parallel realities? Sounds like science fiction."

"Where do you think sci-fi authors get their best ideas? From keeping up with the scientific literature, where else? In any case, Everett and Wheeler suggest constant forking paths in reality—reality, that is, as we know it. As we move down one track, we leave other tracks behind, though they may still continue to exist in other, parallel realities. Perhaps you and I also exist in each of those alternate realities."

"I find that . . . I find that very hard to understand. Hard to accept, too. It's contrary to . . . contrary to every thing we know. Contrary to common sense."

"Of course. The world of quantum reality is bizarre, no escaping that. But it gets even more interesting. Wheeler goes on to suggest that we are in fact *participators*, not just passive *observers* in the development of the physical reality that we experience. In plain language, it seems that reality does not just *happen to* us, but that we somehow play a key role in *unfolding* precisely what form it takes."

"PARTICIPATORS?"

"Wheeler and others suggest that we don't merely stand on the sidelines observing physical reality. Instead, it seems that we participate in the development of the reality that we experience."

"I always thought the world happened *around* me and *to* me. I didn't realize it paid any attention to my opinion on how things should go."

"The world of quantum reality does not choose to conform to our ideas of what seems to make sense. Even those who know it best refer to 'quantum weirdness.' What we do know is that sub-atomic particles, with their own crazy laws, are what constitute atoms, and atoms, in turn, constitute what we perceive as physical reality. Whether we like it or not, or even whether it makes sense to us or not, the laws of quantum reality are laws that permeate our world, as well. As below, in that minute quantum world, so above, in our big, 'normal' world."

He nodded, as if reinforcing what he said. "And one of those laws is that the observer alters what is observed, so that we become participators in reality, not mere passive observers. Hence, by being observers, by selecting the track, we become participators in shaping the reality we experience."

"But it's not in accord with . . . with common sense."

"Exactly. But whether or not our limited minds, operating from our limited experience and perspective, are able to make sense of it is"— he shook his head— "ultimately irrelevant. *Reality is the way it is*, whether or not it makes sense to us."

"But you seem to be saying that no one—not even the specialists in the field—really understands this quantum level of reality."

He nodded. "Largely true, and extremely ironic. Quantum physics explains phenomena not otherwise explainable by other theories. Yet even those who are most knowledgeable in the field themselves cannot understand the quantum world. They can apply some of the principles, but can't explain why they work. Much of quantum reality is still a mystery."

"THE QUANTUM WORLD IS A MYSTERY WORLD, to be sure, but one that has proven to be extremely useful, nonetheless. We have quantum physics to thank for transistors, CAT scans, lasers, and, not to forget, computers. Scientists may not understand why the rules of the quantum world work, but they don't let that stop them from applying the quantum in our technologies."

He paused, eyes twinkling. "Which is much the same as what I suggest to you. We may not understand *why* quantum physics works as it does, just as we may not understand what is behind the Knowledge. But that need not stop you from applying the technology."

"What technology?"

"The Knowledge. The Knowledge is the technology that enables us to join the Reality Track of our choosing."

II   ALL POTENTIAL REALITIES
ALREADY EXIST

❏   The Knowledge teaches us how to use the powers of the mind to shape the way in which the reality that we experience emerges from the sea of undifferentiated possibilities.

❏   The field of quantum physics tells us that until we enter the scene as observers—that is, as we *experience* it—all possible outcomes exist in an "undifferentiated" state.

❏   Undifferentiated—a state in which all is still potential, nothing is settled. All possibilities are out there, latent, waiting for us to settle on the one we experience.

❏   At that point—when, figuratively speaking, we enter the scene—those undifferentiated or latent possibilities reduce to the one which we experience as "actual."

Then "where" does Reality reside?

❏   What is undifferentiated or unsettled?   Everything, absolutely everything—until we enter the equation. The core of all physical reality is nothing more than a sea of latent possibilities.

❏   What we take as our normal physical reality is in a sense an illusion. The ultimate reality is down at the quantum level.

❏   We somehow construct a sense of solidity and definiteness from what is ultimately fuzzy—fuzzy, that is, at the level of sub-atomic reality, quantum reality.

❏   But we cannot ignore that quantum level of reality, because quantum reality is also *our* reality. Those sub-atomic particles—the protons, neutrons and others yet to be discovered—are the building blocks of the physical world we experience.

❏   The "Many-Worlds" approach of Everett and Wheeler (the most widely accepted model for making sense of this strange and paradoxical world), proposes that all possible outcomes of an action exist, each in its own parallel reality.

❏   Everett-Wheeler suggests constant forking paths in reality — reality, that is, as we know it. As we move down one track, we leave other tracks behind, though they may still continue to exist in other, parallel realities.

"Participators," not just observers

❏   Wheeler goes on to suggest that we're actually *participators*, not just passive observers in the development of the physical reality that manifests. That is, that we don't merely stand on the sidelines observing physical reality, but rather participate in the development of the reality that we experience.

❏   It seems that sea of latent possibilities coalesces into the version which we experience as "actual" only at the point at which we humans appear on the scene. Until we arrive to observe it, all apparently remains unformed.

❏   To be sure, the world of quantum reality does not conform to our "common sense" ideas of the way reality works. Even the scientists who know it best refer to "quantum weirdness."

❑   Joining a Reality Track is not so different from changing to a different television program. When we're watching TV, an array of possible TV channels is out there somewhere in the universe. We select the one we care to watch, and it appears on our screen, even though until then we had no human way of knowing it was out there, latent.

❑   In our real lives, an infinite array of possible futures—alternate Reality Tracks—are "out there somewhere," as if waiting for us to join them, latent alternative scenarios for us to step into.

III

THE TRACK WE JOIN
IS
THE TRACK THAT
BECOMES

12

"ALL OF LIFE IS AN ON-GOING EXPERIMENT, an experiment in which we are constantly testing new approaches, and learning from them. Does that make sense to you? Would you agree?"

I nodded. Anything to move him along so I could get to a doctor.

"Perhaps you have not been adventurous enough in experimenting with the possibilities of your life. Have you ever really explored the potentials of your expectations?"

"Explored my expectations?"

"I'm suggesting that you attempt an experiment—an experiment in exploring the limits of reality. Rather, in exploring the limits of what we *perceive* as reality. I'm simply suggesting that you join the Reality Track that leads to the outcome you desire."

Reality Track. There was that Twentieth-Century buzzword again, another of the words he seemed to think of in capital letters. I still didn't know what it meant, nor how it had come to be part of the vocabulary of an old monk in a forgotten monastery.

"How do I do that? How do I join a Reality Track? For that matter, what *is* a Reality Track?"

"'Reality Track' refers to the various potential realities that branch off from a situation. All potential realities already exist, so each of those alternative potential scenarios is what we call a Reality Track. As for how to join a Reality Track? It's really quite simple: *choose* it; *expect* it."

"Just expect it? That's all? But if I don't know what Reality Tracks exist, then how can I choose which one to expect?"

"Suppose you find yourself coming up to a situation in your life, for example whether you will be offered a certain job. Can you forecast the various possibilities in advance?"

"Easy enough: the possibilities are that I get the job or I don't get the job. Or, option three, the final decision is postponed for a while."

"You asked what is a Reality Track? Each of those possibilities is a distinct Reality Track— that is, a potential course in the reality you might experience. Each alternative is a possible scenario of how events might work out from this point forward."

"But how do I, as you put it, 'join' the track I want?"

"Simple enough. You join the track by setting the intention—the *expectation*— that you will step into that scenario. Once you get the knack, you will find it nearly as easy to *join* a Reality Track as to *foresee* it as a possibility."

"But there's a world of difference between sitting back and thinking about possibilities as opposed to having one of those possibilities actually materialize."

"Indeed there is a very great difference. The difference lies in your *expectation*."

"My expectation? What I expect? What I'm hoping for?"

He shook his head. "*Expecting* is more than hoping, much more. And very different. To hope is to wish, while to expect is to *believe, and to act on that belief as if it were a certainty.* Which of course it is."

"Whatever I believe is certain to become?"

"What you believe, or rather expect, *becomes* since it is from your expectation that outcomes result."

"The outcome results from my expectation? What are you saying? That I can shape outcomes—outcomes over which I have no real control—simply by changing my expectations of how things will turn out?"

"To a large extent, yes. But we're getting ahead of things. We should first—"

"Sorry, but I find that hard to believe. *Very* hard."

"It wasn't so long ago that most people found it very hard to believe that humans would walk on the moon. Or transplant hearts. Or do any of the many wonderful things that we now take almost for granted."

"So all I have to do is forecast an array of possible alternatives, select the one I like, and poof! just like that it becomes real?"

He chuckled. "That is an overly-dramatic way of putting it."

"But if it's that easy, why haven't I heard about it before this? Why isn't everybody doing it?"

"Because only now have you found your way to the Knowledge."

"The Knowledge? Those old inscriptions? They tell me how to join alternate tracks in reality?"

"Perhaps if I guide you?"

"I think that's the only way."

"Relax in your chair. Close your eyes. Take a few deep, slow breaths."

I did that. With the soup and bread in my stomach, the wine, the feel of the warm air on my face, it was not difficult to relax, and I quickly found myself floating in a dreamy state, half-awake, half-asleep.

He turned the television on again and flicked channels: soccer, weather, news, then turned it off. "As easily as I've changed channels, you can change the channel in the screen in your mind. In your mind's eye, look at your ankle: what do you see?"

"A very uncomfortable broken ankle that needs to be treated by a doctor."

"Now change the channel in your mind and join a channel in which you see your perfectly healthy ankle. Tell me when you have that image in your mind."

Switching from the fear of how badly injured my ankle was to a feeling of having a healthy ankle wasn't easy. Finally, he broke in to suggest, "Forget about the ankle. Move beyond the problem and see yourself—actually *feel* yourself—walking with no problem and no pain."

An image came to me of walking in the sunshine through a field of soft green grass and bright mountain flowers.

It was about then that I dozed off.

13

I WOKE. Brother Freddie sat across from me, reading from an old leather-bound prayer book. I had no idea how long I'd slept. Sleet still hissed against the windows.

I needed to use a toilet. "I wonder if . . ."

He pointed to a door down the hall. "Thanks to the gift of an earlier visitor, we have indoor plumbing now, after ten or fifteen centuries without."

I was midway down the hall before I realized what I was doing. I was walking. I felt no pain.

I froze in mid-stride, stunned. Before my nap, the ankle had been incredibly painful. Hadn't I even heard the edges of the broken bones rubbing against each other?

Now I was walking on that ankle as if nothing had happened. I lifted the foot off the floor, and rotated the ankle. No pain. I stepped back onto the ground, and put all my weight on that leg. Still no pain.

I heard a sound behind. Brother Freddie stood in the hall, his body shaking with laughter. "A native dance from your country?"

"I don't understand. My ankle doesn't hurt at all now."

"Is that a bad thing?"

"But how can that be? I'm sure it was broken. But even if it was only sprained— well, I've had sprains before, and they take weeks to heal. How long did I sleep—a month?"

His eyes twinkled. "An hour, perhaps not even that."

"How could it have healed in an hour?"

"We can talk about it, if you like."

I glanced out the window. The sleet had given way to big soft snowflakes drifting past. "No better time than the present." I had noplace else to go.

When I returned to the library, I found a pot of tea waiting.

"I don't understand," I said after my first sip. "My ankle was badly hurt—there's no question about that. And whatever the injury was, whether it was a fracture or just a sprain, it couldn't have healed in a couple of hours."

"No? Why not?"

"Because . . . because ankles don't heal that quickly."

"But what if you are now in a Reality Track in which the ankle was never injured?"

"How could I—"

"Or what if," he continued, "ankles normally don't heal that quickly because people have been conditioned to expect healing to take longer."

"But healing in an hour, that's imposs—" I stopped myself. This was the time to listen, not talk. "Was this some kind of miracle?"

"Perhaps your expectations of what is possible are too limited."

"I don't understand."

"The reality you experience reflects the Reality Track you select."

"'Select?' But I didn't *select*—certainly didn't *expect*—to heal this quickly. To tell the truth, I didn't even expect it to heal at all, not until a doctor had treated it."

"Of course you did not expect it, because you had so much wrong conditioning to overcome, so many old habits of mind to get past. I simply guided you in bypassing the limitations that have formed your expectations of what is and what is not possible. Thus your body was freed to mobilize the healing forces within."

"Did you hypnotize me?"

He shrugged. "Names, labels, what do they matter? Call it whatever you will, but I merely talked you past the old expectations that you had built up within yourself."

"But if I was bypassing my expectations—my *experience*—then wasn't I bypassing reality?"

"Ah, but reality is largely a construction of our minds."

14

THE RAIN STOPPED SUDDENLY THEN, and the monastery seemed even more peaceful than before. The sky was still cloudy, though a small patch of blue was opening.

A ray of sunshine cut across the floor. I was still curious about the Knowledge, but felt I'd better seize the opportunity to get away while I could. I jumped to my feet. "Looks like the weather is breaking. I'd better be going now, before it starts again."

Brother Freddie walked to the window and threw it open. Clean cool air, scented with the crispness of fresh snow, filled the room. He beckoned me over.

The clouds blew away as we watched. The mist dissolved, and the village emerged in the valley below, gleaming in the sunshine against the soft green meadows. A rainbow arched between mountain-tops. Already the snow was melting.

But now, for a reason I didn't comprehend, I was reluctant to leave. I knew that I would remember this day all my life, along with Brother Freddie and his gentle ways and his shy, radiant smile.

It had been a special place, and a very special day. I held out my hand. "You've been very kind."

He smiled and nodded. "I was put here to help."

"I need to get to the village before dark, before another storm hits. And I need to—at least *hope* to—find a room for the night."

"May I suggest? Don't just *hope* for a room. Instead, join the track in which the perfect room opens for you. A room in which your missing suitcase awaits you."

"Wouldn't that be nice!"

"Perhaps it would benefit you to attempt another experiment?"

THIS TIME IT WAS EVEN EASIER TO SLIP into that relaxed state.

An image came to mind. I was at a fork in a road, facing several alternatives. I wasn't sure which fork to choose. He said, "Step into the track that leads to the outcome you desire."

"But how do I know which track leads to a room?"

"You don't need to choose the track. Rather, focus on the *end*—on where you ultimately want to be. "Join that perfect outcome, let the track bring you to it."

"I still don't—"

"Do you see the room you want?"

"I can picture a room in my mind's eye, if that's what you mean."

"Is that truly the perfect room for tonight?"

"Forget about perfect: I'll be satisfied with anything at all, at this point. It wouldn't have to be anything special, just a place to sleep."

"Why limit yourself? Why not select a perfect room while you're about it? There's no point in being self-limiting from the start, is there?"

"A *perfect* room? Oh no, no. I wouldn't want anything very luxurious. I'm here on a limited budget."

"I'm not suggesting luxury, I'm suggesting that you select the perfect. There is a difference. Select the room that's perfect for you, that's perfect for this situation. Now tell me about that perfect room. How will you recognize your perfect room when it appears? What does it look like, how is it equipped, what kind of view does it have?"

That took some thinking. "A big soft bed with a cozy down comforter. A modern bath. A balcony looking out over the meadows and mountains."

"That room awaits you. Now see—"

"A room awaits me? How can you be sure of that?"

"Because all possible outcomes already exist. You need only join the track that leads you to it. Now see your luggage in the room. More than just *picture* the bag, *know* that your bag is there waiting for you. But you must do more than just wish for it, you must *expect* it."

It was all imagination, so I went along and envisioned my bag on a little stand just inside the door. Oddly, for just an instant the image was so real I felt as if I were actually standing there in that room. For that instant, it felt as real to me as any room I'd ever been in. It was like *remembering* the room, not just *imagining* it.

"That room and that suitcase are there for you. Join the track that leads you to them. Expect them, and hold that expectation. What you expect is—with high probability—what you will experience. You selected to step down a certain Reality Track. Now keep yourself on that track. Hold a clear, focused intention that you will encounter your room and your luggage at the end of that Track."

"Clear focused intention?"

"Hold a clear mental image of precisely what you would have. Don't waver, don't doubt. Expect that outcome."

"I'll try."

"*Mere trying* isn't enough. You must *expect*. With full confidence."

15

"NOW IT IS TIME FOR YOU to go down to the village and claim your room, along with your suitcase. Otherwise, the good people there will think that you have been lost, and come looking for you. This monastery is always the first place they look, naturally."

"I wish I had your confidence. The fact is, my suitcase is probably somewhere on the other side of the world."

"That possibility does exist," he said. "Indeed, all possibilities already exist in potential form. The issue is, which track in reality are you choosing to join? When you toy with unpleasant possibilities, you risk having your intentions misunderstood."

"Misunderstood? By whom?"

He shrugged. "By whomever. By whatever." He paused a moment, before adding, "If I may say so, perhaps the problem of your life is that you have spent too much of your energies focusing on the tracks that lead to where you *do not* want to be."

Too much of my energies—and of my expectations— taking me to where I don't want to be. That did seem to make a lot of sense. Still, I hedged by saying, "I'm just being realistic."

"Ah, but *is* it realistic? Reality, after all, is largely a construction of our minds. Keep our experiment in mind: you have chosen to join the Reality Track leading to a perfect room, along with your suitcase. Now you must do your part by stepping into the track that leads you there. It's counter-productive to be distracted by negative possibilities."

I CHANGED INTO MY OWN CLOTHES, dried now by the warmth of the fireplace. Brother Freddie walked with me back the way we had come, down to the kitchen, then along the enclosed cloister to the little chapel where it had all begun.

He paused at the chapel door, his hand on the knob, as if to open it. I expected that he would take me back into the chapel and explain the inscriptions—the Knowledge—before I left.

Then he let go of the knob and turned away from the door. "No, I think it would be best to wait for another day to talk more about the Knowledge. For now, it's best for you to experiment, trying for yourself things we've discussed today."

"You haven't actually told me what the Knowledge is," I reminded.

He nodded. "Quite right, quite right, you have not yet been introduced to the inscriptions that codify the Knowledge. We will talk of them, I promise, but another day. Today has been very full for you, and the day is not finished yet. Now you need to get down to the village, and begin seeing how your experiments turn out."

He shook my hand vigorously with a hand that I again found surprisingly strong and calloused for such a small old man. "You are always welcome here, of course. I expect you will be back."

He winked as he said the word "expect," and that made me wonder if he meant it as a statement or a question.

It had been an interesting day, but also a very strange one. I wondered how I would feel about this later, after a night's sleep.

In any case, it seemed unlikely that I would be coming back to the chapel. Even if I wanted to, how would I ever find the path? Would I have to take another tumble off the main trail to find it again?

HE CALLED ME BACK. "Remember, keep your sense of expectation strong. *Expect* it, not just wish it. And don't let your confidence waver."

16

I PAUSED ON THE WAY DOWN to savor the view of the little village nestled against the mountains. This truly was the fulfillment of a dream to be here. Too bad that Jackie had passed up the opportunity.

Brother Freddie had called me back a second time,   this time to suggest that I try still another experiment: to join the track that would enable me to make it back to the inn before more rain hit. As it happened, for most of the journey down the mountain I walked in late afternoon sunshine.

It seemed that I had indeed made it back to the village without a problem until I rounded the last bend. A gust of wind hit me in the face, and I smelled rain in the air.

Hold the expectation, I reminded myself as I jogged through the village, racing the storm, and made it to the little inn where I'd spent the previous night. I was barely inside the door when sheets of rain swept down the street and hammered at the windows.

At least that part of the experiment worked out: I got here ahead of the rain. Now came the test of the next experiment: would the inn have a room for me, after all?

An older woman, someone I had not seen before, staffed the front desk now.

She wagged her index finger when she saw me. "No room, all gone."

"I had a reservation," I tried again.

She spoke only the local language, and shook her head that she didn't understand.

I printed my name on a piece of paper. She looked at it and something seemed to click in her eyes. I wondered if there was a problem. Rather, a new problem.

She opened a file folder and leafed through the sheets. She stopped at one and read my name aloud. There was something in the way she said it that made me think she was upset about something.

"That's me," I said, pointing to my name on the sheet.

She lifted the telephone and dialed a number. She seemed angry. Or was I reading too much into it? I couldn't see her expression as she hung up the phone, but she pointed to a small sofa by the door. "You sit."

I sat. A couple of minutes later, I heard a car pull up outside. The front door opened, and a pair of uniformed policemen stepped in. The woman behind the desk pointed to me.

The policemen walked over to stand in front of me, one on each side. "You come now," the older one said.

"But—"

"Come."

They opened the back door of the police car, and I climbed in, thinking, Once one thing goes wrong, everything goes wrong. And, There's no situation so bad that it can't get worse.

Then a thought struck me, and I found myself laughing. It *did* seem that the experiment was working out, after all, and I *would* have a place to sleep, after all . . . but a place that was not very comfortable.

Maybe I should have been more clear in precisely what Reality Track I was selecting.

17

"THE TAXI IS AWAY ON A CALL," the manager at the new inn told me, after the police dropped me there. "Our village is small, and the police help visitors when that happens."

"Do you have a room for me? For tonight?"

"You have a room here for as long as you care to stay." He was at least 70, with a cherubic pink face capped by a thatch of snowy-white hair, and a thick white moustache that obscured most of his mouth. The amplitude of his stomach was a promise of the good things to come from the kitchens of the village.

He led me up the staircase, then opened the door wide as if raising the curtain on a stage. The room was magnificent, far beyond anything in the travel brochures I'd studied at home.

The glass doors opened onto a balcony with a view across the village to the mountains beyond. Church bells chimed the hour. The bells reminded me of the chapel up on the mountain and Brother Freddie. As crazy as his "experiment" was, at least I had a room.

I tested the bed: the mattress was as soft as a cloud, and the sky-blue eiderdown comforter would mold to my body, leaving me toasty-warm in the cool night air.

"It's perfect, a perfect room," I told the innkeeper.

Perfect. As I said the word, Brother Freddie's words echoed in my mind: "How will you recognize your perfect room when it appears?"

That took some thinking. "A big soft bed with a cozy down comforter. A modern bath. A balcony looking out over the meadows and mountains."

This room was almost exactly what I'd pictured—the down comforter, the modern bath, the balcony, even where the bed was positioned in relation to the balcony! Bizarre.

A coincidence, of course, it couldn't be anything more than that.

The innkeeper bowed, and closed the door behind himself as he left. Then I saw my suitcase waiting by the door, just as I had envisioned it.

I felt a chill move up my spine. Still *another* coincidence. By now, wasn't I way over my quota of coincidences for one day?

I HAD TIME FOR A HOT BATH before dinner, and finally got a good look at my ankle. I was sure I'd felt the broken bones grating when I first arrived at the monastery. Now, just a few hours later, the ankle seemed fine.

There was only one logical explanation: I'd been cold, frightened, and disoriented after the fall. I'd lost consciousness—maybe had a minor concussion. Obviously, in that state of stress, I'd imagined the sound of the grating bones, and mistook mud on the ankle for swelling and bruising.

Afterwards, I bundled up and sat on the balcony, struck by the sight of the snowy mountain-tops glowing orange in the last of the sunset.

The day, as I looked back on it, already seemed surreal, as if the time in the little chapel had been a dream.

So far, all aspects of the "experiment" Brother Freddie suggested had worked out to my benefit. I had "expected"—or was it "selected?"—to make it to the hotel before the rains returned, and I did make it just in time.

I had "expected" to have a room waiting, and a magnificent room turned up, almost precisely as I had envisioned it.

I had "expected" my luggage, and it was there when I arrived.

But could I have somehow *caused* these events to fall into place by my "selecting" or "expecting" them? Now that I was back down the mountain it was obvious how little sense that made. Wishing for something doesn't make it happen— that's Reality 101.

The events—the rain holding off, the room opening up, and the suitcase arriving—were just coincidences, they *had* to be just coincidences. Lucky breaks for me, but still just chance happenings, nothing that I could have brought about by "selecting" them.

Brother Freddie meant well, and certainly believed in his so-called Knowledge, whatever it was. But now that I was back in . . . well, back in the *real* world, it was clear enough that my wishing—or expecting—couldn't make things so.

In the real world, what we select does *not* become—not unless we *make* it happen, and that means working up a sweat and getting your hands dirty, not just sitting on a mountaintop "expecting" good things to just fall into place.

My suitcase had probably been delivered hours before Brother Freddie had begun prodding me to "expect" it, so how could there be any possible link? You obviously can't cause something to happen if that event has already taken place.

To settle my mind, I phoned down to the front desk to ask when my suitcase had been delivered. "A few minutes before you arrived. It came in on the five o'clock train."

"When did the room become available?" I'd been told that the whole village was booked solid for weeks ahead.

"Also a few minutes before you arrived. A gentleman decided to cut his stay short and go back on that same train."

A LUCKY COINCIDENCE, it seemed.   But *was* it just a coincidence?

Another lucky coincidence that the room happened to look so much like the one I'd envisioned?

Still another coincidence that my suitcase had been waiting by the door—as I'd envisioned it?

And that I had made it to shelter just before the rain hit?

And, of course, that my ankle wasn't bothering me now?

But that added up to a long string of coincidences.

18

I SHOULD HAVE KNOWN BETTER than to phone Jackie. Our last few conversations at home had been strained, but I wanted somebody to talk to.

"I hope you're having a good time," Jackie said with no enthusiasm, "but you were very foolish to have gone ahead with this trip. You should be back here now, trying to line up another job."

I passed that over, and talked of the journey, of losing my bag and my hotel reservation, of getting lost on the mountain and of finding my way to the chapel and Brother Freddie.

I tried to explain his ideas of selecting Reality Tracks, and the experiment he suggested, and how the things I had selected in that experiment—getting a hotel room, and finding my suitcase waiting—had come about.

"The whole idea is totally absurd, and you know it. You were simply lucky. And speaking of luck, you're stretching that luck by not being here looking for a job. While you're frittering away time climbing mountains and sitting in old chapels, keep in mind that somebody else is here grabbing the job you need."

I tried to lighten the mood. "When I get back home, I'll select a Reality Track that leads to a perfect job."

"It's not going be a *perfect* job, don't fool yourself. Just a job, *any* job, will do. Besides, I know you're talking like this just to annoy me. That's not the way things work—as you used to realize. If you want something, you have to fight for it, and you're not here fighting."

"But—"

"In any case, I must go now. This call is costing money, and money—as you once seemed to realize—is finite. Besides, I have a big presentation to make tomorrow."

"A presentation, and you're unprepared for it? That's hard to imagine." Jackie was a control freak who over-prepared for everything, and then prepared some more.

"Of course everything's ready. But still something could go wrong—as I'm sure it will. You may have your new philosophy, but I still live by what I've always believed: Expect the worst, and once in a while you'll be pleasantly surprised."

III   THE TRACK WE JOIN
IS THE TRACK THAT BECOMES.

❑   All potential realities already exist; each of these alternative potential scenarios is what we refer to as a Reality Track

❑   How to join a Reality Track? Simply *expect* it. Join the track by setting the intention—that is, the *expectation*—that you will step into that scenario. (Once you get the knack, you will find it nearly as easy to *join* a Reality Track as to *foresee* it as a possibility.)

❑   Step into the track that leads to the outcome you desire. Focus not on the *track*, but on the *end*—where you ultimately want to be. Join that perfect outcome, and let the track transport you to it.

❑   Hold a clear mental image of precisely what you would have. Don't waver, don't doubt. *Expect* that outcome. Intend it to come about, with total confidence—or "faith."

❑   All possibilities already exist in potential form. The issue is, which track in reality do you choose to join? (Caution: When you toy with unpleasant possibilities, you risk having your intentions misunderstood.)

❑   What you expect is, with high probability, what you will experience.

But if . . .

❑   But if we bypass our expectations—built upon past experience—aren't we bypassing reality?

❑   Ah, but keep in mind that reality is largely a construction of our minds.

❑   So perhaps our expectations of what is possible have been too limited, because we have failed to understand the potential of the larger reality in which we exist.

❑   Perhaps our expectations are too limited because we have so much wrong conditioning to overcome, so many old habits of mind to get past.

IV

WHAT MAY SEEM TO BE UNUSUAL COINCIDENCES ARE MERELY NORMAL HAPPENINGS IN A DIFFERENT REALITY TRACK

19

THE MORNING BROKE SUNNY AND CLEAR, with an azure sky and crystalline air.

I stepped out onto the balcony, and gazed across the rooftops of the village to the velvety green meadows carpeting the foothills, spotted with the colored dots that were cows and sheep. The vista of snow-capped mountain tops glistening in the morning sun nearly took my breath away, and I felt as happy as I could ever recall being.

A church bell in the distance tolled the hour. The scent of hay blended with the aromas of flowers warming in the morning sun.

After a hearty breakfast, I headed out of town on the same trail as yesterday, determined to finish the walk I'd begun before the storm and my detour to the chapel.

I did feel a pull to return to the chapel, partly because I was still curious about the inscriptions. But I decided against it. It didn't seem likely that I'd ever get the chance to hike these mountains again, so the sensible thing was to take advantage of the good weather and explore while I had the opportunity.

Besides, yesterday had been a magical day, and I wanted to leave it just as it was in my memory. "Good things only come our way once"—one of my father's sayings.

I was at the lookout an hour up the mountain when I saw the first cloud. What if the rain hits again? I wondered, the memory of yesterday's driving sheets of rain flashing through my mind.

I tried to push away the image, but it stayed with me, and the rain began a half-hour later. Today I had my waterproof hiking boots and my rain gear, and I pushed on.

The rain got heavier, then changed to sleet that stung my face.

"Am I having fun?" I asked myself, then headed back to find the path to the chapel, feeling a strange sense of inevitability, as if this was the track that I had joined somehow on the deeper level of my mind.

I STEPPED INSIDE AND CALLED OUT. No reply. I pulled off my rainsuit and found an old wooden hanger by the front door.

Brother Freddie stepped out of the shadows, again as if materializing from the stone walls. He carried a tray with two mugs of steaming tea and handed me one, inviting me to sit with him on one of the wooden pews.

"You must have seen me coming," I said, grateful for the hot tea.

He chuckled. "To tell the truth, I did expect you." Again, as yesterday, he winked as he said "expect," as if he and I were sharing a private joke.

"'Expected me,' you say?"

He smiled and shrugged, but said nothing.

He'd worn a rough brown woolen robe yesterday; today his robe was orange. I asked him about it, for something to fill the silence. "Is there a significance to the color? Something in the church calendar?"

He shook his head. "Nothing liturgical, only a gift from a monk of another tradition who passed through once. We exchanged robes to symbolize our exchange of ideas."

"Do you get many visitors?"

"People find their way here when it is appropriate for them."

"Are there other monks here?"

"I am the only one now. But when it is time, another will come forward as Keeper of the Knowledge."

"Are you part of an order?"

"Perhaps. But the records have been lost. Only the Knowledge remains."

20

"I SEE THAT TWO OF YOUR EXPERIMENTS were successful," he said.

"Experiments?" Then it came to me: he'd led me through that supposed experiment yesterday, trying to set me onto the Reality Track that yielded my suitcase and a good room for the night.

He laughed, probably at the shock he saw on my face. "How do I know the experiments were successful? By a process no more mysterious than noticing your fresh clothing. And, I should add, by noticing that you look rested and well-scrubbed: evidence enough that you found a room."

I had to laugh along with him. Sherlock Monk. "As it happened, there had been a cancellation, and a room turned up, one even better than what I'd reserved. And my suitcase did happen to come in on the evening train."

I should have left it at that, but the way he sat silently, as if waiting for me to go on, unnerved me, and I blurted, "But I think it would be unrealistic to attribute that to anything more than mere coincidence."

Immediately I regretted saying it.

I expected him to show anger, or maybe sadness. Instead, he chuckled and said, "'Mere coincidence,' you say. Is that such a bad thing?"

"Oh no, of course not. But you can't count on coincidences when you need them."

He nodded, as if I had come up with the right answer. "You're absolutely right. If you don't expect what seem to be coincidences to come along when you need them, then of course the probability is that they will not. What we expect, after all, is what tends to happen."

"How do you tell the difference between—" I groped for the words. "Between something that's the result of 'joining a track,' and something that's a mere coincidence?"

"A mere coincidence?" He shook his head. "I'm not sure that there *is* such a thing as 'a mere coincidence,' the universe being, as it is, all of a piece."

It didn't seem that he'd grasped my question. "My point is, how can I be sure that what seems to result from a coincidence is actually the result of my selecting a Reality Track, and not just something that would have happened anyway?"

He laughed, but I didn't see the joke. I was puzzled, but with Brother Freddie it was hard to be offended by his laughter.

"You're asking how you can prove whether or not the outcome in fact resulted from your selecting a certain Reality Track. What kind of evidence were you anticipating? A thunderclap to announce that a room had turned up for you? Perhaps the sound of trumpets to herald the sight of your suitcase flying in through an open window?"

Even I had to laugh. "Nothing like that, obviously. But . . ." I couldn't finish the sentence, because I didn't have any idea of what kind of evidence could possibly convince me of the ability to cause coincidences to happen.

He shook his head. "That's good, because in all my years, I've never heard trumpets announce anything. A few thunderclaps, yes, but those only to announce that my expectation of a storm was being fulfilled."

"Then how can you be sure it actually is anything more than a coincidence?" I asked again.

"What happened with you is typical of the way things come about when you select a Reality Track. Things don't materialize out of thin air, and they rarely announce that something special is happening. It's usually more subtle. What *appear* to be coincidences fall into place. But they turn out to be *meaningful coincidences that perfectly fit the context*, and provide the perfect idea or information or introduction at the perfect time. Yet they seem to arrive as normal happenings. And they *are* normal, once you have stepped into the Reality Track in which they are meant to occur."

21

"BUT WISHES DON'T COME TRUE!" I said.

"Absolutely right," Brother Freddie said, nodding vigorously. "Mere wishes don't come true, no doubt about that."

"Then . . . then what are we talking about?"

"The difficulty is in translating the Knowledge into language that's meaningful in today's vocabulary."

"But what *is* the Knowledge? You still haven't told me that."

"Yesterday was not the time. Perhaps now is." Sudden concern passed over his face. "Provided, that is, that you are ready for the consequences?"

"What consequences?"

I was cranky by then, annoyed at having a second day disrupted by the rain. Yesterday had been an interesting experience, one I didn't want at first, but something I wouldn't have missed for anything. But my time in the mountains was limited, and now I wanted to be out on the trails, not sitting inside playing mystery games with an odd little monk.

Without replying, he walked to the altar and knelt to say a silent prayer. I wasn't sure whether I was expected to join him. I decided not to. At this point, the only thing I'd be praying for was good weather so I could get back onto the hiking trails.

He pulled himself to his feet, using the altar railing as a brace, then walked over to the stone wall. His difficulty in getting back to his feet made me realize how old and frail he really was—a reality otherwise obscured by his energy and good-humor.

Yesterday the stone wall of the chapel had seemed to be covered with a mass of carvings. Now I saw that they broke into eight distinct rows. Eight sentences? Eight clusters of some strange code?

Brother Freddie paused by the wall and looked at me, and again I felt that some inner part of me was being appraised. "Do you recall what I said yesterday when you first asked about these carvings?"

"Something about my life would change?"

"I told you yesterday that if you once absorb and learn to live by the Knowledge, then your life will change. Forever. Are you ready for that?"

The silence hung heavy in the air. Did I really want my life to change—forever? My life was certainly not perfect, not as happy or as fulfilled as I'd hoped it would be. But it was the only life I had. Did I dare to mess with it?

Still, that life didn't seem to be going anywhere—certainly not any place that I wanted.

Something else he'd said yesterday came to mind: People find their way to the Knowledge when they are most totally lost. Maybe there *was* truth in that. It was obvious now that I *had* totally lost my way in life before I stumbled upon this chapel yesterday. Maybe it *was* time to try a new direction.

"Yes," I finally said, "I'm ready for the Knowledge. I'm ready for a change."

"Good. Very good." He turned to the wall, hesitated, and turned back to me. "I think it would be best if I translate into the modern vernacular."

"I beg your pardon?"

"The Knowledge was inscribed in another time, in a very old language. As I said, some of the expressions and vocabulary are difficult to translate without making allowances for today's usage. The fine line between 'select' and 'expect' is one example of the difficulty. We have, in fact, already discussed the first three principles of the Knowledge."

He reached up, standing almost on his tip-toes, and pointed to the words carved into the rock as he translated.

NOTHING IS AS IT SEEMS.

"That reminds us that physical reality is deceptive. Things are not as solid as they seem. Indeed, everything on this earth is made up of atoms, and atoms are made up of sub-atomic particles, along with a great deal of empty space. Everything around us may seem solid, but in reality everything is 99.99% empty space. Some physicists even suggest that there is no such thing as matter, that all is ultimately energy."

He reached up and pointed now to the second inscription, translating it, as,

ALL POTENTIAL REALITIES ALREADY EXIST.

"The findings of quantum physics are helping us understand this. Common sense and everyday experience conspire to convince us that there is only one *now,* and only one way events play out."

He paused, giving me time to think that through. It seemed obvious enough, so what point was he making?

"But our physicist friends tell us that isn't necessarily the way things really are. They tell us that all potential outcomes already exist, though in a latent form. At a certain point, when we humans arrive on the scene, that array of latent possibilities compress to one actual outcome—a concept expressed by the Knowledge as,"

THE TRACK WE JOIN
IS THE TRACK THAT BECOMES.

There were still a few more lines of inscriptions carved into the rock. But I had a pressing question that I couldn't wait to ask.

22

"THAT'S IT? THAT'S THE CORE OF THE KNOWLEDGE?" I blurted, then immediately hoped I hadn't offended him.

"Perhaps you are thinking that these few words carved on an old church wall can have no real impact?"

"Something like that."

"Einstein wrote even less—$E=MC^2$—and changed the way the universe was perceived."

"But $E=MC^2$ was"—I groped for a way to express it—"was only a symbolic way of expressing a much larger concept."

"Then why do you assume these messages convey less?"

"WHAT DOES IT MEAN?"

"What do you think it means?"

"That whatever I wish for—rather, whatever I 'join'—comes to be?"

He pondered that a moment, then said, "That could be a way of expressing it, yes. The Knowledge does offer us the option of selecting those courses in reality that we encounter."

"Are you telling me that I can just choose to have things work out the way I want? Are you telling me that I can switch tracks in reality as easily as I would change railway trains?"

"Even more easily than changing trains. When you change Reality Tracks, there's no need to carry your baggage from one car to the next."

He let me absorb that, as incredible as it seemed, then he added: "Though there is one small footnote I must add. This physical world in which we live is one of *probabilities*, not *certainties*. The Knowledge provides a way of greatly increasing the probability of experiencing desired outcomes."

"So it's more like, 'The Track We Join is the Track we will *Probably* Experience?'"

He sighed. "The difficulty is in the meaning of the word 'probability.' Bear in mind what I said yesterday. The findings of quantum physics reveals that there is no certainty in this physical world, only probabilities."

That had been when I first arrived, stressed out, and he'd said there was only a probability that the atoms in the stones of the chapel would stay in their anticipated orbits.

"As I said then, this talk of probabilities is nothing more than a way of looking at reality, though looking at it from a different perspective. The probabilities favor the stones remaining intact, just as the probabilities favor your strong expectations coming to be. The Knowledge, I repeat, provides a way of greatly increasing the probability of experiencing desired outcomes."

23

"SO WHEN I WOKE FROM THAT NAP yesterday and found that my ankle didn't hurt—"

I broke off, not sure how to phrase the question. "If I understand what you—rather, what the Knowledge is saying—the reason it didn't hurt any more was that somehow I'd joined another track in reality. Are you suggesting that I joined some kind of parallel world in which my ankle had not been injured?"

"That could be the case. We just don't know. And when I say 'we,' I'm referring not just to the two of us, but even more to the best scientific minds around. At this point, they can't explain many of the principles of quantum physics, but they find that the principles *work*, regardless of whether or not they understand why."

"But what happened to that original world, the world in which my ankle was broken?"

"Good question, though it brings us back to the issue of what happens to all of those television programs that you *don't* turn on:

do they collapse out of existence, or do they continue in another reality in which you're not watching them?"

"I had to think about that. If we carry that possibility through to its logical end, then isn't it possible that there might be another alternate world in which I do have a broken ankle, and I'm still trying to get down the mountain?"

"What happens to that other version of reality? We don't know. All we know from our experience is that there's a kind of shift—often evidenced by what seem to be strange coincidences coming about to change the course of events. At that point, apparently, you have joined that other version of reality."

He went back to the stone wall and pointed to the fourth inscription as he translated it:

WHAT MAY SEEM TO BE
UNUSUAL COINCIDENCES
ARE MERELY NORMAL HAPPENINGS
IN A DIFFERENT REALITY TRACK.

"BUT IF I JOINED A DIFFERENT REALITY TRACK, A DIFFERENT UNIVERSE, why didn't I feel it at the time?"

Brother Freddie shrugged. "I don't know. No one knows. I think not even Dr. Everett and Dr. Wheeler can explain that one. But what really matters is not so much the theory as the fact that you *did* join the Reality Track in which you have a perfectly sound ankle."

He had a point. Maybe I should just accept my good ankle as a piece of good fortune, and not question my luck. But I was still curious. "If—*if*—it was real, I want to know why."

"Don't we all? But there's a saying among the scientists and engineers who are working on practical applications of quantum theory— people who are developing things like MRI scanners and fantastic new generations of computers. The motto they live by is, 'Shut up and compute.'"

"Meaning?"

"Meaning, we don't understand *why* it works, but it *does* work, so let's get on with the job of using it productively."

"So I should just quit trying to find why, and just expect perfect outcomes?"

Brother Freddie nodded. "Now you're getting it. Maybe someday we'll understand the why, but in the meantime let's just use the Knowledge to help make this a better world. Let's just shut up and expect the perfect track."

24

"SHUT UP AND JOIN THE PERFECT TRACK? But how can I know what that perfect track is? How can I be sure that it even exists?"

"All potential realities already exist."

"So it's just out there somewhere, and I don't have to worry about where, I just somehow step into it?"

"You told me you didn't know where the various television signals were, yet when you touched the remote control, there they were, as if waiting for you all the while.."

"But television programming is virtual reality, just electrical signals that a TV tuner converts to an image. I didn't have a *virtual* ankle, I had a *real* ankle, and it was hurting."

"There's less difference than you might think between the virtual reality of a TV signal and the physical reality we share. A television signal is just energy waves, translated by an electronic device we call a tuner into something on a screen that our eyes can pick up and send to the brain to be 'constructed' into a sense of reality. You translated moving dots on the TV screen yesterday into what you perceived as a soccer match."

"I'd never thought of it that way," I said, for something to say. For that matter, I'd never even thought of it at all, I'd just taken it all for granted.

"Now look at the leaves out on the trees. What color are they?"

"Green."

"But there is no such thing as 'green. You're not seeing green leaves, your eyes are picking up electromagnetic waves of a certain length that corresponds with what we *call* green, and your brain is translating those waves into something of the shape, size, and color of what we call tree leaves."

"SO JOINING OTHER REALITY TRACKS isn't so very different from changing television channels?"

"The difference is, you don't need a remote control to join other Reality Tracks."

"But how do I do it? How do I learn to join these other Reality Tracks?"

"Can you tell me how to learn to ride a bicycle?"

"Tell you how? I can't tell you—that's something you can only learn by doing."

"Is it difficult?"

"At first it is. Sometimes you fall off. Then you get the knack of it and you find you're rolling, and then you practice until your skills build and it becomes automatic."

Brother Freddie smiled. "That's precisely how to learn to use the Knowledge. Try it. Experiment with it. Sometimes you'll succeed on your first attempt. Other times, you'll fall and get up and try again. Slowly the skill builds until it becomes automatic, and joining other Reality Tracks seems a perfectly natural thing to do."

25

"JOINING MIRACLES! That's what you're really talking about, isn't it? You speak of joining 'Reality Tracks,' but you're actually talking about joining miracle tracks!"

He chuckled. "What is a miracle?"

"What's a miracle? You're the clergyman, you're the expert on miracles. You tell me."

"But it was you who used the word."

I shrugged, trying to think. "Something special, something very special. Extraordinary."

He reached into the pocket of his robe and pulled out a well-worn little dictionary, opened it to a page marked by a small slip of paper, then fished out a pair of small, wire-rimmed reading glasses, which he adjusted on his nose until he had the distance just right.

Then he read, "A miracle is 'an event or effect in the physical world deviating from the known laws of nature.' Or, an outcome that 'transcends our knowledge of these laws.'"

He looked up at me, then echoed what he had just said: "Miracle: an effect that transcends—goes beyond—our knowledge of the laws of nature."

"So the Knowledge really *is* about joining miracles?"

"It could be said that the Knowledge does in fact provide a way of, as you put it, 'joining miracles.'" As he said the words, he raised both index fingers to set them off in mental quotation marks. "That is, joining what *seem* to be miracles, but may in fact be normal operations under laws we don't yet understand. 'Miracles,' as St. Augustine said, 'happen, not in opposition to Nature, but in opposition to what we know of Nature.'"

I found myself nodding, shaking my head, and shrugging—all at the same time. How do you carry on a conversation about miracles?

He smiled, "So, yes, in the sense of a miracle as an outcome that transcends our very limited knowledge of the apparent laws of the physical world, then indeed we *are* talking about the possibility of joining miracles."

26

"BUT IF THIS IS REALLY POSSIBLE, then why isn't everybody already doing it? Why isn't everybody 'joining miracles' all the time?"

He shook his head. "It's been my experience that 'everybody,' as you say, follows what 'everybody' else does. 'Everybody' assumed that it was impossible to run a mile in four minutes. Then Roger Bannister did precisely that in 1954, and, ever since then, 'everybody' has known that a four-minute mile is indeed possible. Now it's almost commonplace."

"But miracles — I always thought of miracles as from some higher dimension. It doesn't seem right to classify setting a record in a footrace as a miracle."

He shrugged. "In the view of the experts of the time, before Bannister, a four-minute mile was completely out of the question, something utterly beyond the physical limits of a human being. Therefore, that first four-minute mile transcended the laws of nature—as they were then known. Bannister's achievement fit the definition of miracle: 'an event in the physical world that deviates from, or transcends, what we believe to be the laws of nature.'"

"But it wasn't a real miracle, just a case of some experts underestimating the capabilities of a well-trained individual."

"Exactly so! But is there a difference?"

"I don't follow."

"Perhaps it is not only in the area of athletics that we underestimate human capabilities. Perhaps, if we would only allow ourselves, we could transcend in other ways what we take for granted to be the limits of the possible."

"Are you suggesting that I could work miracles—if I'd only 'allow' myself to do it?"

"It goes back to the Knowledge. The track we join is the track we expect. By consciously focusing our expectations, we bring about the reality track that we experience. But one must join that track. *Join* it, not merely wish, not just hope for it."

═══════════════════════════════════

IV   WHAT MAY SEEM TO BE UNUSUAL COINCIDENCES ARE MERELY NORMAL HAPPENINGS IN A DIFFERENT REALITY TRACK

❑   How do you tell the difference between something that's the result of 'joining a track,' and something that's a mere coincidence? Perhaps there *is* no such a thing as 'a mere coincidence' . . . at least not on things of any importance.

❑   How can you be sure that what seems to result from a coincidence is actually the result of your selecting a Reality Track, and not just something that would have happened anyway?

❑   Things don't materialize out of thin air, and they rarely announce that something special is happening. It's usually more subtle. What *appear* to be coincidences fall into place. But they are *meaningful* coincidences that perfectly fit the situation, and occur as seemingly normal, random occurrences.

❑   And they *are* normal, once you have stepped into the Reality Track in which they are meant to occur.

❑ But if you really do join a different reality track, a different universe, why don't you feel it at the time? No one knows.

"Shut up and compute"

❑ How does it work? No one really knows, not even the people who are working on practical technological applications of quantum theory. They work by the motto, "Shut up and compute," Meaning, "We don't understand *why* it works, but it *does* work, so let's get on with the job of using it productively."

❑ It's the same with our application of the principles in our lives. Maybe someday we'll understand the why, but in the meantime let's just use the Knowledge to help make this a better world. Let's just shut up and expect the perfect.

Is it a miracle when we join a more perfect track in reality?
Ah, but what IS a miracle?

❑ Joining miracle tracks? But then the question comes, What is a miracle? One definition: A miracle is "an event or effect in the physical world deviating from the known laws of nature."

❑ Another definition: "An outcome that 'transcends our knowledge of these laws.'" In short, think of a miracle as an effect that transcends—goes beyond—our knowledge of the laws of nature.

❑ Then again, when we "join miracles" we may be proceeding in normal operations under laws we don't yet understand.

❑ St. Augustine: "Miracles happen, not in opposition to Nature, but in opposition to what we know of Nature."

❑   So, in the sense of a miracle as an outcome that transcends
     our very limited knowledge of the apparent laws of the
     physical world, then indeed we *are* talking about the
     possibility of joining miracles.

❑   Perhaps it is not only in the area of athletics that we
     underestimate human capabilities. Perhaps, if we would
     only allow ourselves, we could transcend in other ways what
     we take for granted to be the limits of the possible.

V

THE PRESENT TRACK EVIDENCES PAST EXPECTATIONS

27

"BUT IT'S JUST NOT POSSIBLE! There's no possible connection between what I 'expect' or 'select' or 'join' and what occurs in the world outside my direct control."

Brother Freddie wagged his finger. "Perhaps it would be more accurate to say that there is no *apparent* connection. Even better would be to say, '*there is no link detectable by our present methods.*'"

"No matter what you call it, the fact remains that there's simply no possible way my thinking could impact outside reality!"

"Ah," he said, raising one finger, "but what if it *IS* true? What then?"

I didn't realize then how that phrase would keep nagging at me for days to come. "What if it is true? What then?"

"Ah," Brother Freddie said, again, raising that one finger, "but what if it *is* true, what if what happens on the sub-atomic level *does* relate to what happens in our world? What if the human mind *does* impact matter? What then?"

"WHAT IF THE KNOWLEDGE IS RIGHT?" he continued. "What if the conventional wisdom is wrong? It wouldn't be the first time. The conventional wisdom claimed that the earth was the center of the universe. The conventional wisdom insisted that the earth was flat. The conventional wisdom scoffed at the idea that there was such a thing as germs, or that sanitation made a difference. The conventional wisdom said that it was absurd to think that man might fly, then the wisdom said that it was ludicrous even to suggest that man might fly to the moon. The conventional medical dogma decreed that stomach ulcers were caused by stress, and the establishment laughed when a pair of Australians proposed that bacteria was the cause, not stress and acid. It took a couple of decades of struggling against the conventional wisdom before minds opened to that new idea. Now those Australian rebels won a Nobel Prize for their insight—and their tenacity."

"But—"

"Now the conventional wisdom rejects the idea that there might be more to humans than the instruments of today can measure. But what if the conventional wisdom is wrong, once again?"

"IS THERE SCIENTIFIC EVIDENCE to support this? You've talked about the theories proposed by quantum physicists, but they're just theories. What solid evidence is there?"

"They are theories, that is true. But those theories, or 'mental models,' or 'maps,' or 'hypotheses,' flow from what has been found to be true at the quantum level. The theories are attempts to make sense of the strange phenomena that occur at that level."

"But things that happen in a lab, events that are only perceptible to an electron microscope or a super-collider . . . they're all well-and-good," I said. "But, frankly, I'm not convinced that they have any bearing on the real world. I mean, suppose an electron does make a quantum leap to another orbit, well, so what? That doesn't make a bit of difference in my trying to get another job, or . . . or on anything in the world in which I live!"

Brother Freddie nodded, then said, "Again, I ask, But what if it *is* true, what if what is true on the sub-atomic level is equally true in our world? What if the human mind does impact matter? What then?"

28

"INDEED, ASKING WHETHER THE KNOWLEDGE CAN BE PROVEN in the manner of today's science is, I believe, the *wrong* question."

"Then what *is* the right question?"

"*Does the Knowledge work for you?* When all is said and done, is that not what really matters?"

I paused, expecting another trap. "I suppose so." That did make sense. But it didn't feel right. "Still, I'd feel more comfortable if there were some science behind it."

"Of course," he nodded. "But tell me: what is science?"

"Science? Why it's . . ." I floundered, suddenly realizing that it's one of those words you know until you try to define it.

He reached into his pocket for his battered little dictionary and antiquated glasses, then read, "'Science: accumulated knowledge systematized and formulated with reference to the discovery of general truths or the operation of general laws.'"

"But I think of 'science'—real science—as research, experiments, that sort of thing. Form the hypothesis, conduct experiments to test it, revise, refine the experiment, test again."

"Exactly so: research and experiments—the raw material of true learning. But I ask you: what better experiment than your own to test the reality around you? What better research than an examination of the archives of your own life to discover the ways in which the Knowledge has already operated for you . . . or against you?"

"*Already operated?* But how could it? I've only just heard about the Knowledge, so how could it have already operated for me?"

"There are two ways of coming to an understanding of the validity of the messages within the Knowledge. One is to experiment for oneself in applying its lessons. To that end, you ran some experiments last night, with apparent success."

I wasn't convinced that a room and a suitcase happening to turn up was enough evidence to settle the issue, but I wasn't about to argue that now. "What's the second way?"

29

"THE SECOND WAY OF TESTING THE KNOWLEDGE is to examine the ways in which it has already operated in your life."

"But, as I said, how could the Knowledge have already operated if I've only just now heard about it?"

"Look at where you are in your life—particularly the situations that are most significant at this point. Then trace back from them to find what your actual expectations *must have been* in order to bring about those outcomes."

"It sounds like looking at an answer to figure out what the question must have been."

He nodded. "Indeed so. The Knowledge says, 'The Track We Join is the Track that Becomes.' This sixth principle is a corollary of that:"

THE PRESENT TRACK EVIDENCES
PAST EXPECTATIONS

"In other words, given the fact that you've arrived at this present situation, what must have been the expectations that placed you here?"

He paused, peering at me, apparently to be sure I was following him, then added, "In other words, What does where you are *now* tell you about what your expectations must have been in the past?"

"THAT'S NOT TRUE, NOT TRUE AT ALL! It *can't* be true!" I said when I grasped the implications.

"And why is that, my young friend?"

In "young friend" I felt a gentle rebuke. Perhaps I was over my head. Or perhaps I was reading more into it than he meant.

But I pushed on. "We've already been through this. The events that have been coming into in my life lately are pretty rotten. There's just no way I'd ever have 'selected' to have things turn out the way they have."

"You think not?"

"Or is the Knowledge saying that I'm so stupid and masochistic that I'd have chosen to have most everything go wrong for me?"

His eyes were calm, but I was sure that I must have offended him. So be it. He called himself the Keeper of the Knowledge; let him defend his Knowledge. If he could.

I went on, "Or is it that—just as I've always said—'Once one thing goes wrong, you can expect everything else to go wrong, too?'"

I was surprised at the anger I heard in my own words. Maybe I shouldn't have been surprised. I wasn't just angry about having a hike rained out. My real anger was deeper: looking back now, I can see that I was angry at life and at the way things had been going for me.

It wasn't Brother Freddie's fault, but he was there at that moment and got the brunt of it.

The damage was done, so I continued: "Is the Knowledge suggesting that I *selected* to have things to go wrong in my life? Is it saying that I got fired because I *wanted* that? That I *wanted* my wedding to fall through?"

I pulled myself to my feet, ready to get out of there. Then I added, "I don't care what your Knowledge says, there's just no way on earth that I'd have selected those things to happen. I needed that job. I wanted that marriage."

HE RAISED HIS HAND. I stopped, the force of the sudden anger spent. He said, "What if, on another level of your mind . . . ?" He let the sentence hang unfinished, and seemed to wait for my response.

"'Another level of my mind?' You're not suggesting that, somewhere deep down inside, I actually wanted to lose my job, and then somehow sabotaged things in order to bring it about that way? That's just not—"

He cut in. "Did you want to come to the end of that job?"

"Of course not." Then I added, "I mean, it wasn't a perfect job, but at least it paid the bills."

"Was that work how you ultimately desired to spend your life?"

The question caught me by surprise, and I had to think about it a moment. "Was that how I wanted to spend my life? Not at all. I hated the work from the start. The fact is, I'd been wishing for years that I could make a change. But work is work. You're not supposed to like it."

I added, "But I definitely did not want to lose the job. Not now. Not without something else lined up. Not when I was about to get married."

"But you do agree there was at least a part of you that desired to be out of the situation?"

Again my own response shocked me: "Sure, I miss the security of having a steady paycheck. But now that I've been thrown out of the situation? Frankly, what I'm really feeling now is a sense of relief."

I took a deep breath, then admitted, "Okay, I suppose there was a part of me that wanted out, no question about that."

The absurdity of it struck me. "In fact, now that I'm away from it, now that I have time to think about it, I'm not just *relieved*, I'm *delighted*. Getting thrown out of that job really was what . . . well, I suppose it's what I *would* have selected. If I'd only had the courage."

I thought again, and added, "But I wouldn't have chosen getting fired as the way to do it."

"Not consciously, no. I'm sure you did not consciously choose it. Nonetheless, it is instructive to explore the possibility that you slipped into this track by your unconscious expectations."

30

"LOOK BACK OVER THE WHOLE PATTERN OF YOUR LIFE to understand what tracks you joined, as evidenced by where they have carried you," Brother Freddie had said.

As I sat on the balcony before dinner, I did just that.

From my chair, I saw the last of the sun, now gleaming orange on the snow-caps of the mountains. In the villages further down in the valley, dusk had already set in, and the lights sparkled on, one by one.

But what I saw when I looked back over my life was not so pleasant. If the Knowledge was correct, and we do indeed "Become" the track we select, then it was clear from the fix I'd gotten myself into that I had been selecting and expecting the wrong things in my life.

As I left the chapel, Brother Freddie had given me a card, on which he had printed, *"What does where I am now tell me about the selections and expectations that have placed me here?"*

Now, the more I thought about it, the more the events of my life rolled past, the more clearly I was struck by one very unsettling reality: in my life, in my career, in my relationships with Jackie and others, even in the little day-to-day things—*I had gotten exactly what I had expected: the mediocre, the disappointing, the unfulfilling.*

Life had not been as good to me as I'd have liked. But the fact is, I had not *expected* life to be easy or fulfilling or lucrative. What I had expected was struggle, setbacks, tough going—and those are precisely what I had encountered.

I'd developed a pattern of coming close but never quite getting the really good jobs or the good promotions.

Coming close but not quite winning or succeeding was, now that I looked back, just about what I'd come to expect of myself.

I'd seen myself as diligent and hard-working, but someone who, when all was said and done, always fell just a little bit short, forever snatching failure from the jaws of victory.

THEN I SUDDENLY UNDERSTOOD. I was *not* a failure, not at all! The fact was, *I had been overwhelmingly successful in virtually every aspect of my life!*

What is a failure? Someone who fails to achieve what they set out to accomplish. By that definition, I had *not* failed. To the contrary, I had succeeded totally: *I had achieved precisely what I had expected for myself.* I'd been getting mediocre pay in a mediocre job, for which I was given mediocre recognition.

I had *expected* mediocrity, and had *successfully achieved* mediocrity. I had expected struggle, expected difficulty following difficulty on a road to ultimate futility—precisely what I experienced.

Instead of consistently *failing*, I had consistently *succeeded*—succeeded in achieving my *actual* expectations. However, since my goals had been only mediocre at best, and negative at worst, I had succeeded in achieving outcomes that were not really desirable, not what I really wanted . . . but were exactly what I had expected.

I REALIZED THAT IN MANY INSTANCES I had never dared to expect good things to happen. Actually, I had often not even let myself *want* them.

Why was that? I wondered.

I concluded after some thought that I had never dared to want good things to drop into my lap because my twisted mindset held the view that to *want* something was to risk failure. So, by *not wanting* success, I had succeeded in failing.

I could see now, in the light of the Knowledge, that by not allowing myself to want, and then to expect, I had all but guaranteed that I would get nothing better than whatever happened by chance to come along for me.

31

A CHURCH BELL TOLLED THE HOUR as I walked to a restaurant. I thought of Jackie, who was missing out on this experience.

Up here in the mountains, infused with insights from Brother Freddie and the Knowledge, I was beginning to see Jackie with fresh objectivity.

Jackie was always struggling, forever looking for problems and slights. Ironically, despite all the fretting and worrying and playing out worst-case scenarios, Jackie also had that knack of consistently managing to extract doom from any circumstance.

It struck me then how Jackie lived with the expectation of disasters, foul-ups, plots, conspiracies, competitions and scarcities. And, invariably, they manifested, just as expected.

Brother Freddie's words echoed in my mind: "Reality, as we think we know it, is largely a construction of our minds." It occurred to me just how much Jackie's negative mindset foreshadowed the reality that seemed to emerge.

It struck me, too, how strongly that mindset had infected me during our time together. In the years before we met, I'd had a good many advances, along with a reasonable share of setbacks. Overall, I was comfortable; certainly not living up to my potential, but still comfortable and moderately successful.

My career progress had been mediocre, merely average. But at least its direction had been upward in a slow—very slow progression.

Then Jackie "educated" me on the need to anticipate problems and troubles. From that point, things seemed to change, and the more I worried and fretted and become drawn into that nexus of diminishing possibilities, with dangers around every corner, the more I lost my upward momentum in life.

Now my progress had halted. By the time I left on this trip, everything had gone wrong, to the point that I was out of a job, and facing the prospect of a slide back down the hill that I had so slowly and painfully climbed.

Did that happen just by chance? Or was there something to Brother Freddie's idea that the reality I encountered had been largely a construction—or was it a selection?—of my mind and my negative expectations?

Was it because I had come to *expect* problems and setbacks as the norm that they had *become* the norm?

Could it be that my *expectation* of problems had been *drawing* problems to me?

IT WASN'T JUST JACKIE'S INFLUENCE THAT PULLED ME DOWN.

We called my old boss "Mr. Worries." He was not yet 40, but could pass for twenty years older, and now I began to understand why. He *looked* for problems, he *expected* problems, and, not surprisingly, he *got* problems. And the problems were wearing him out.

He and I commuted together, and I came to know a man beset by problems with his marriage, with his children, and, I deduced, with his finances.

But it was at work that I directly encountered the troubles that he seemed to provoke.

Those problems came as a surprise, because, until he took over the section, things had worked fairly smoothly. It was only after his arrival that things spiraled downward

To take one instance, we'd never had any difficulties in getting supplies on time. But from the time he took over, he was obsessed with the possibility that delivery delays would upset our schedule. The old hands tried to reassure him that we worked with reliable firms; there was no need to worry. His response: "We need to be prepared for contingencies. What if those suppliers aren't really as good as you think?"

It was no coincidence (I see now, from the perspective of the Knowledge) that before long exactly the kind of delays he feared began occurring. Suppliers who had never missed a shipment began missing once, then a couple of times each month.

"See what I told you?" he'd exult then. "You've got to plan for worst-case. Expect worst-case and be ready for it, and maybe once in a while you'll be pleasantly surprised. Once in a great while, things actually will work out as planned."

KAREN HAD BEEN A FRIEND since high school. I had bumped into her a few months ago. I knew that she'd had a difficult first marriage, and it seemed the second was turning out to be even worse. We'd been friends long enough that I felt I could ask what she could do to correct the situation.

"Not much. Actually, nothing at all. I don't want to make waves." Then I thought she was going to cry. "I just want to get by, just survive till the end. That's all I want, all I've ever asked out of life: just to get by."

Now, given the insight of The Knowledge, the outcome was predictable: If all she wanted was to get by, then that's exactly what she would get. She would get by, and get nothing more, entrapped in the track she expected for herself.

AND THEN THERE'S MY FRIEND GRANT. The older Grant gets, the more he seems to making a career of operating below his potential. His life has been dominated by financial fear.

Afraid to spend money, he'd been notoriously frugal, living cheaply, making do, reluctant to invest even in necessities. It showed: he spent as little as possible on clothing and housing, and his cars were always a step away from the junkyard.

The result? Intelligent and talented as he was, he looked shabby and second-rate.

Besides, he was unwilling to extend himself, or to take any kind of risk. He stayed in that first job for years, even though it offered no pathway for advancement. But it was safe. "I suppose I could do better," he once said, "but if my boss ever found out I was looking, he might fire me, and then I'd have nothing at all."

That was the pattern of his life: avoid risks, stay with the sure thing, the bird-in-hand. Hold tight to what little you have because you'll probably never get as good again—and certainly nothing any better.

Ironically, Grant has suffered more setbacks and disasters than anyone I know.

The track we select is the track that becomes—and bad news if that track is one of fearfulness and scarcity.

MY REVERIE WAS BROKEN by the arrival of two couples who settled at the next table. I couldn't help overhearing their conversation.

"We always set high expectations for our son," one of the men said, "and he always met and exceeded them. From the time he began school, we made a point of letting him know we believed in him and what he was capable of. He never let us down."

"He wasn't perfect," the wife said. "But, then, none of us are. We're only human. But John knew that we trusted him, and he lived up to that trust."

"Well, you were certainly lucky to have had the child you did," the other woman sniffed. "You had one you could trust. Our daughter wasn't like that, at all. She was a rebellious child from the start. We warned her, we disciplined her, we pushed her, we told her how hard her life would be if she didn't get an education . . . and look how she ruined things for herself."

32

HAVE A BANANA BEFORE BED and you'll have no trouble sleeping—a life-lesson from my aunt, who at 90 is still popping with energy.

I'd been too weary by the end of my first couple of days here to need any help sleeping. But I wasn't so tired tonight, and it seemed a good idea to have a banana or two on hand, just in case.

But I soon found that wasn't going to be easy. The waitress said that by now all the shops in the village had closed for the night, and the restaurant had none on hand.

Another good opportunity to experiment in applying the Knowledge. While I waited for the bill, I closed my eyes and envisioned myself stepping down the Reality Track that led to one little shop, somewhere in the village, a shop that hadn't yet closed, a shop with a supply of nice fresh bananas, bananas just the way I like them, with a trace of green so they're almost crisp on the inside.

I wandered the quiet streets of the little village, "Expecting" to find that shop still open.

I was already picking up from Brother Freddie that tendency to set off words in mental capitals. To "Expect," in caps, had come to mean to *will* something to come about. "Expect," in caps, implied *intending*, which was very different from "expecting," as predicting, wishing, or plain hoping.

Some shops with bright windows full of clocks and chocolates and colorful sweaters and calendars were still open, but none of the food shops. That old song came to mind: "Yes, we have no bananas today."

Hadn't I seen vending machines in the railway station when I arrived? Maybe, just maybe, I'd find a banana there with my name on it.

My hunch paid off: the station was open, there were vending machines, and—incredibly—one of the machines held a nice small bunch of bananas with that perfect hint of green.

As I slipped my last coins into the slot, I heard that familiar little voice inside me whispering, "Just watch! Whatever can go wrong will go wrong. These are your last coins, so you can be sure the machine will let you down."

The coins tinkled down the slot, and I pulled the latch of the door leading to the bananas. It didn't release. I tugged again. Nothing.

I felt the old frustration, the old self-pity boiling up inside me. I wanted to kick the machine, to slam it up against the wall until it gave me back my money.

Then something occurred to me: The Track We Select is the Track That Becomes.

The Reality Track I selected had indeed led me, not to a shop, but instead directly to bananas. Perfect so far.

So maybe I'd left out one aspect of that Reality Track. I wanted not just to *see* a banana, but to *hold* one and *eat* it.

I stood there, looking at the bananas just beyond reach, trying to figure how Brother Freddie would play it from this point.

Why not experiment again? Maybe there was still a way I could step into the Reality Track that actually put a banana in my hand.

I hadn't pushed the coin release button, so the final outcome wasn't locked in yet. In one Reality Track, the machine would keep both the bananas and the coins. In the other Track, it would give me back my money, so I could try again.

I paused a moment, consciously selecting the Track that led to holding the bananas in my hand.

Then I reached down and pushed the coin release button, anticipating the tinkle of my coins as they rolled down into the cup. Nothing.

I pushed the button again. Still nothing.

I turned and walked away, giving up. Yes, we will indeed have no bananas tonight.

So much for the experiment, I thought. There is no certainty in this physical world, Brother Freddie had warned, only probability. And tonight the probabilities had not been with me.

THE HOTEL WAS QUIET WHEN I RETURNED. I was beginning to feel a bit sleepy. Maybe I wouldn't need bananas, after all.

I went out onto the balcony for one last view of the mountains, then came in and pulled the drapes before getting ready for bed.

That was when I noticed the basket of fruit on the dresser.

Along with some pears, grapes, and three perfect bananas, I found a note from the village tourist bureau, apologizing for the "error" that had resulted in the loss of my hotel reservation the other evening, and hoping that this basket of fruit "would in some small way make up for the inconvenience."

I ate one of the bananas, and slept till a rooster crowed to signal morning.

33

I SLEPT WELL, BUT DREAMED OF HOME AND MY FAMILY.

What we expect, becomes, and an immense part of what I expected had been shaped by the messages and examples I'd received at home.

I'd had—until my visit to the little chapel—very limited expectations of what was possible in my life. I'd expected to hold a small job with small pay and small satisfaction, and of course that had come to be.

I had expected life to be precarious and difficult, and so it had been.

I had expected the love relationships in my life to be (I grope for the words) practical not passionate; a partnership, not a friendship; a working relationship, not a loving relationship. And so they were.

In the months since my return home, I'd often wondered from whence had come those limited, negative expectations. Until my visit home, I'd figured that they must have sprung from within myself.

But once I got thinking about the people I'd grown up with, parents, siblings, relatives, I realized that a lot of these limiting expectations had been programmed into me from childhood, from the things my parents said, as well as from the ways they lived their lives.

They'd grown up in times when things really were hard. The economy had long since outgrown those conditions, but my parents had not—nor had the people with whom they spent most of their time. Some people talked sports, other people politics or the things they had seen on their travels. Not my parents and their friends. Their conversations centered on how bad times had been, and how things were sure to get even worse before long

I suppose it was inevitable that kind of mindset had become implanted in my own view of the world, and from those core inherited beliefs I'd built my own batch of further self-limiting expectations.

Don't misunderstand me: I don't blame my parents. Not at all.

But now at least I do *understand* them: they became what they expected.

Their own expectations were limited and negative, and hence became self-fulfilling prophecies, and the reality they lived was of limitation, difficulty, unhappiness. They became victims trapped in their unhappy expectations, and inevitably passed on that world-view to their children as naturally as they passed on the tendency to walk on two legs.

MY FATHER WAS OLD FOR HIS YEARS, worn down by constant struggle. He'd always worked hard, and didn't mind working. But he never got a promotion that I can recall, or much of a raise.

But it wasn't the hard work that wore him down, it was coping with what he saw as constant internal politics and struggles. "It's a tough, cruel world out there," he would tell us at least once every week. "It's everyone for himself. You can't trust anyone, especially the people you think are your friends, because they'll be the first to shove the knife into your back. That's the most important thing you've got to remember when you go to work, because if you don't keep your guard up, you'll find somebody else eating your lunch every damned day. People like us, we never get the breaks, we're just the little army of ants that do the work. Do what you have to do on the job, then pick up your paycheck and get the hell out when quitting time comes. And then just hope the job hasn't dissolved under your feet before next payday."

MOTHER IS A SWEET SOUL, but, I see now, afflicted by expectations equally as low as Dad's, though not bitter and negative—just resigned to limitations.

She had grown up in poverty (so she believed at the time, though I'm now seeing that the real poverty was of aspiration and expectation).

As a child, she lived in perpetual hand-me-downs, and in later life never bought anything new for herself. Most of her clothes were either from her sisters or from the Nearly-New Shop. The household products and tools she used were always the cheapest—and I can tell you from experience that those pennies do make a difference. Inexpensive cleansers may cost less, but they take a toll in extra effort. Cheap foods take their own kind of toll.

But even now she won't treat herself to upgrades. "It was good enough in the past, no sense changing now. Who knows when we'll need the extra money" is still one of her mantras.

Another is, "People like us need to learn to be satisfied with what we have; we can't expect the best."

Still another: "Thank the heavens we got through this day with no new disasters, but I dread what tomorrow will bring."

AS LOW AS THEIR EXPECTATIONS WERE FOR THEMSELVES, their expectations for their children were even lower.

In a sense, that made for less stress on us. They never expected us to do well in school, so we felt no pressure to excel. "None of our children are brains," we heard often, so often that none of us invested the effort in pushing for the top.

They didn't expect anything from us, and certainly never communicated any sense of what their idea of success would be for us. Since we didn't have any targets to aim for, we were never quite sure if we were successful, or if we were behaving properly. Or even if we were loved. If I brought home a report card with all B's, Mom and Dad would look it over and nod and sign it and send it back. It was the same with report cards that had mostly D's. I didn't get punished for poor work, I didn't get rewarded or even praised for what other parents would think was good work. So before too long I settled on doing only the minimum to get past the teachers.

To this day, I still don't know whether I have managed to live up to what my father and mother had hoped for from me.

Now, looking back, I suspect they never had any dreams or expectations fo They were resigned to taking whatever fate dealt out.

V   THE PRESENT TRACK EVIDENCES
PAST EXPECTATIONS

❑   How can there be any possible connection between what we "expect" or "select" or "join" and what occurs in the world outside our direct control?

❑   Perhaps it would be more accurate to say that is that there is no *apparent* connection.

❑   Even better would be to say, "there is no link detectable by our present methods."

But what proof exists? Has it been scientifically proven?

❑   Good questions, to be sure. But perhaps asking whether the Knowledge can be proven in the manner of today's science is the *wrong* question.

❑   Be open to a better question: *Does the Knowledge work for you?* When all is said and done, is that not what really matters?

❑   What better scientist than yourself for experimenting in the reality around you? Test for yourself. Do these principles work for you?

❑   Beyond that, examine the archives of your own life to discover the ways in which the principles of the Knowledge have *already* operated for you . . . or against you.

❑   Look at the situations in which you find yourself, and ask, Given the fact that I have arrived at this present situation, what must have been the expectations that placed me there?

❑   In other words, *What does where I am now tell me about what my previous expectations must have been?*

But what if?

❑   Beyond even the issue of whether these principles can be proven in conventional ways, or even whether we can ever understand why or how quantum physics "works," is the issue of, *What if it IS true? What then?*

❑   What if what happens on the sub-atomic level does relate to what happens in our world? What if the human mind does impact matter? What then?

VI

THE BECOMING
MAY BE
AN OPENING DOOR

34

I SET OUT ON A DIFFERENT PATH the next morning, and visited the glacier for which the village is famous. On the way back that afternoon, I saw a marker for a side trail to the monastery. That seemed like a good idea, particularly as my legs were feeling very heavy.

Today in the sunshine, Brother Freddie was outside working in his garden. Instead of a monk's robe, he wore an old flannel shirt and a pair of work pants, muddy in the knees. He face again broke into a smile when he saw me. "Ah, my young friend! You arrive just in time to give these old bones an excuse to take a rest."

In place of the usual hot tea, today he offered cool water hand-pumped up from a well. We settled in the shade of a grape arbor, and I told him about the insights that had come last night.

He listened, not saying much. I expected that sooner or later he'd suggest we move into the chapel. But he did not, instead sitting silently, apparently thinking something out.

Finally he looked up and said, "It sounds like you had an interesting day yesterday, but I sense that you still have concerns. Perhaps you would like to talk about them?"

I TOLD HIM ABOUT THE BANANAS last night, and how I had unsuccessfully "selected" to find a shop open, and then how I had "selected" to buy bananas from the vending machine, and how the machine wouldn't cooperate, instead keeping them tantalizingly just out of reach, behind glass.

And then the irony, after all that, of finding that bananas had been waiting for me all the while back in my room.

He chuckled. "Einstein once said that he did not believe that God plays dice with the universe. But at times it seems to me that God does play small jokes."

It struck me that this was the first time he had used the word God. A monk who didn't talk of God?

"SOMETHING PUZZLES ME," I said.
 "Yes?"
 "You're really a monk?"
 "Yes."
 "But I always thought of monks as, well, *religious,* if you know what I mean."
 At that, his head rolled back and he laughed loud enough to startle the pair of birds that had been feeding in his garden. "And you think that I am not? Define religious."
 It took some thinking, and I still couldn't come up with a real definition. "All I can say is you're not like most of the clergy I've ever known."
 He chuckled. "That's been said of this monastery before." He shook his head. "Not always was it meant as a compliment."
 Then his face turned serious. "But tell me, why do you think that I am less than normally 'religious?'" Again he raised the first two fingers on each hand to mark his mental quotation marks.
 I was regretting I'd gotten into this. "I haven't been here that much, so I don't really know what you do the rest of the day. Maybe that's when you say your prayers."
 "One's entire life is a prayer—assuming, of course, that one lives with that perspective."
 "Another thing: you're a monk, yet when you referred to the idea of God playing jokes—that was the first time that I've heard you use the word God."
 "I did speak of the One, your first day here, your first few minutes, in fact."
 "The One is God?"
 "The One, the Universe, the Force, the Source, the Creator, the Divine, the Lord, the Name, the Ineffable, Yahweh, Allah, Providence, Great Spirit, Divine Spirit, That From Which All Comes, Home, God, *Deus, Dio, Gott, Dieu, Dios,* the Great Power, the Power of Powers, the Root of all Being, the Cause of Causes, the Ultimate, That Which is Beyond All Understanding—to mention a

few. God answers to many names, to more names than we could ever imagine. And yet—"

He paused, and I finally asked, "And yet what?"

"And yet it is such a tragedy that factions battle over names and descriptions of what they cannot begin to comprehend. You have heard the story of the three blind men who try to describe an elephant?"

"Remind me."

The first blind man felt only the trunk and insisted the elephant was a great snake. The second felt only the leg and was convinced it was a great tree. The third felt only the ivory tusk and said that the elephant was a polished stone."

"I have heard a version of the story, a long time ago."

"Yes. But now suppose that instead of merely disagreeing, each of these blind men was so certain that his understanding, and only his understanding was correct, that he was prepared to fight the others to the death? Presumptuous, is it not?"

I had to nod in agreement.

"That is why I sometimes simply use the term TWIBOC."

"TWIBOC? I've never heard it before. Is it a word? An acronym? Something from another language?"

"TWIBOC—That Which Is Beyond Our Comprehension. Or, if you will, That *Who* and so forth."

"So that's another, your own, term for—what, who we might call God?"

"There are people who say they don't believe in God, or who claim to be angry at God. But they can't tell you who or what the God is they're rejecting. But that's the reality—our human minds cannot comprehend what that God-force or God-power or God-mind is. Hence I tend to use the term, 'That Which is Beyond Our Comprehension.'"

I pondered that a bit, then said, "But those people will say they do know God, or at least what God is described to be."

"But who describes God? Who can, if they're honest, truly claim to be able to describe the infinite."

I really didn't have a response.

"Do you like flowers?," he asked. I assumed he was changing the subject.

"Sure, who doesn't?"

"Do you know flowers by name—which are roses, which are lilacs, which are dandelions?"

"Those I do. Along with tulips and poppies and some others."

"Do you know *all* the flowers of the world?"

I had to shake my head. "Of course not. I doubt if anybody can. I'm missing your point."

"Why can't any one person know all the flowers of the world?"

"There are just too many, an immense number of them. It would take an immense number of lifetimes to travel to see and study them all."

"Can anyone describe all those flowers?"

"How could they, if they haven't seen them all?"

"My point exactly. If that person has not seen or sampled all the flowers of the world, then they could not honestly describe them, at least in anything more than very broad terms."

"And your point is?" I thought I knew, but wanted to hear him say it.

"If we humans can't even describe the flowers of the world, how could any of us honestly claim that we can define and therefore limit That Who or Which Is Beyond Our Comprehension?"

"FOR A MONK, for a clergyman, you're very flexible. Incredibly flexible."

"Flexible?"

"You're not, well, dogmatic, rigid like, well, like so many others I've . . ."

He shrugged. "Perhaps 'realistic' is the word. As God has many names, I think also that God's house has many doors."

"What do the other monks, the officials, think of you—of this monastery?"

"There are no other monks here any longer. I am the last."

He smiled, "As for the officials, as you call them, "I believe they think nothing at all. It seems that we've been forgotten over the years. Perhaps that's just as well."

35

"IS THE KNOWLEDGE FROM GOD?"

"All ultimately is from the One."

"But did God, the One . . ." I stammered, not sure of what question I was trying to ask.

"Did God personally carve the inscriptions into these walls?" he said, then shook his head. "I don't know. The answer is, Probably not. But then I am, after all, only human. How can I presume to limit God?"

"But there's no mention of God in the inscriptions. Or does that come in the parts you haven't talked about?"

"The One—or God, if you use that name—permeates the Knowledge, as the One permeates the universe."

"But you haven't spoken much of God. Or the One. Or any of those other names for . . . well, for God, the Divine."

"We yearn for God and the spirit, but we are not always ready."

"Meaning?"

"Sometimes it's best not to begin at the beginning."

"Meaning?"

"Suppose we'd had this conversation that first day when you found your way to the chapel?"

I pondered that a moment. "To be honest, I'd probably have tuned you out, thinking it was the same—" I cut myself off before I let the words slip.

"Thinking it was, as the saying goes, 'the same old stuff?' Is that it?"

"Something like that," I admitted.

"Sometimes it is helpful to come from a new direction, to intrigue."

Now I had to laugh. "And in order to intrigue me, you talked about quantum physics, one of the most intimidating subjects on earth?"

He smiled, shrugged, and pulled himself to his feet. "Enough rest. I think now the time has come for us to get back to work." He hobbled along the flagstone walkway to the door of the little chapel, then pulled it open, signaling me to enter.

He retrieved his brown robe from the rack and shuffled it on, then approached the altar and again knelt in prayer.

Today I knelt beside him, but no prayers came to mind. My mother had taught me some, but that was a long time ago. Even back then, they had seemed to be just words we mumbled—just going through the motions.

HE WALKED TO THE CARVINGS ON THE WALL.

"Again, we pass over the first inscription for now," he said, then pointed to the words as he reviewed the two inscriptions we had covered yesterday:

THE TRACK WE JOIN
IS THE TRACK THAT BECOMES.

and,

THE PRESENT TRACK EVIDENCES
PAST EXPECTATIONS.

"As we said yesterday, perhaps you might relate better to the second message if you think of it as, 'We become entrapped in the tracks we have selected.'"

He paused, then asked, "Any questions?"

I shook my head. There were a dozen questions, maybe a hundred I could ask, but I figured that the best thing was to move on and cover all of the inscriptions. Then I could put my questions into context. Maybe even all of my questions would have been answered by then.

He nodded, then turned back and pointed to the words of a new message:

THE BECOMING MAY BE
AN OPENING DOOR.

He let me absorb that, then he said, "The way your bananas manifested last night provides as good an illustration of the principle as any. When you 'select'"—again he raised his fingers to throw quotations around the word—"when you 'select,' sometimes things work out precisely when and how you anticipate. Other times they come in unanticipated ways and times . . . and sometimes in unanticipated forms. You told me that you first selected to find a shop open, then selected to find the bananas in the kiosk at the railway station."

"There were bananas there, but I couldn't get to them. They were locked away behind glass. Very frustrating."

He smiled. "That raises the question of whether your expectation was broad enough. What we—"

"I'm not sure what you mean by 'broad enough.'"

"Did you develop a clear focused intention of *possessing* the bananas, or only of *seeing* bananas?"

"It makes a difference?" I *had* thought of that last night, so maybe I was on the right track to learning.

"It could. It's one thing to see bananas, which might belong to someone else, and quite another to have your own, which you are free to eat. That's why your intention must be clear, so that you step onto the Reality Track that leads to precisely what you want."

He started to speak, then paused, then started again. "For much the same reason, it's important to *focus on the end that you would achieve, rather than the details of how you would get to that end. Your* idea for achieving the objective might not be the *best* way. If you're too specific on the how-to, then that how-to could get in the way."

"This is getting complicated."

"Not really. The main point is clear: The track we select is the track that becomes, so clarify what it is you ultimately would have. *Remember: develop a clear, focused intention of what it is you ultimately want. Focus on the important end, not the interim steps.*"

"THIS NEW MESSAGE—The Becoming May be an Opening Door—would translate in today's usage as something on the order of, 'Be patient, as your selection may not come at once.' Or, 'Be flexible and creative, as it may take vision to recognize what arrives in a different form than you anticipated."

An expression of delight passed over his face, and he pulled another index card from the pocket of his robe. "Hmm! I never thought of putting it quite that way before," he mumbled, then sat on one of the wooden pews and printed on the card, using a pen he pulled from still another pocket.

I expected him to hand me the card. Instead, he held onto it, and said, "There's another implication that flows from this message: *a setback may be a signpost.* The fact that something doesn't work out just when and how you had anticipated . . . well, that's a cue to go back and look again. That apparent setback may be a signpost sending you in a new direction. What appears to be a failure or a disappointment may be a new, wholly unexpected Reality Track opening up."

It struck me at that moment that perhaps the breakup with Jackie, painful as it was, could be just this kind of signpost. Provided I was open to it, and creative and flexible enough to recognize it when it did come.

It would be nice, I thought. But it seemed far away.

"LOOK FOR THE DOORWAY—that's another implication flowing from this message."

"Doorway? What doorway?"

"When your expectation doesn't seem to manifest, there's almost always a doorway. Find that doorway, even in what appears to be a solid wall, and it will open to an even better way of achieving the end you're seeking."

"That sounds nice." Which, as I said it, sounded patronizing. But Brother Freddie didn't seem to notice.

HE PRINTED a few more lines on the index card, then pulled himself out of the pew. If I had to guess his age, I'd put it well into his '80's. My knees were hurting from the day's hike: what must his old knees be feeling like after a day's gardening?

He handed me the card, then pulled off his robe, hung it on the wooden hanger, and held the door open for me to precede him out.

"I don't mean to rush you, my young friend, but I know you have a distance to go yet this afternoon, and I have some more work to do in the garden while the weather is favorable. Besides, I expect you'll be well-advised to get down the mountain at a certain time."

The phrasing puzzled me. "At a certain time? Is something going to happen?"

He grinned. "I expect so."

"'Expect' as in 'select?'"

He shrugged and held out his hand, an impish grin on his weathered old face.

36

I TOOK A NEW PATHWAY DOWN THE MOUNTAIN, a shortcut Brother Freddie suggested when I mentioned that my knees were tired after the long day's hike.

Even better, if I made it in time, the final bus of the day would carry me the last three miles to the village.

True, I had come to the mountains to hike, but there comes a time when some pampering is in order, and if ever there was a time to pamper my aching knees, along with my tired legs and burning feet, this was it.

At last I emerged from the forest onto the main road, and spotted the bus still waiting at the stop.

I waved, and started to jog, no small feat in hiking boots and a pack.

A massive logging truck came around the bend, creeping on the steep grade. Then the truck driver touched his air brakes, and waved to the bus to pull out ahead.

"No! Don't leave! Wait for me!" I yelled, waving my arms.

But it did no good; the bus drove off without me.

I walked on, my legs even heavier after the jogging. How could that happen? I asked myself. Was the bus driver so stupid he forgot to look in his mirror? He saw the logging truck, why didn't he see me?

Or was he so rigid that he'd pulled away at the exact second, according to the schedule, despite a passenger who was already in sight?

I felt the old dark mood coming back upon me, that mode of self-pity and resentment toward the world.

I thought I'd selected a nice, comfortable bus ride. What went wrong? Had I somehow failed to select "hard" enough? Or had I selected on one side of my mind, while the other side sabotaged the selection by expecting to be foiled again?

THEN I RECALLED TODAY'S MESSAGE: The Becoming May be an Opening Door.

What was there to open for me? The insight that my knees, tired as they are, can take still more abuse?

Hardly that.

I recalled the impish grin that Brother Freddie wore as I left today. Something was up — I was sure of that. But what? How, exactly, had that conversation gone?

"I expect you'll be well-advised to get down the mountain at a certain time."

"At a certain time? Is something going to happen?"

"I expect so."

"'Expect' as in 'select?'"

He hadn't answered. Had he selected this, for me to just miss the last bus of the day? Fine friend he was.

THERE WAS LITTLE TRAFFIC ON THE ROAD, once the bus and logging truck had disappeared from sight. It seemed that the chances of hitching a ride were somewhere between zero and none.

Clouds emerged from behind the mountain, and a light sprinkle quickly developed. A little rain was no real problem, now that I had my rain gear. But it was just one more little thing. Was I back to the bad old mode where once *one* thing goes wrong *everything* goes wrong?

Or was there some kind of positive "Opening" from the "Becoming" that had begun with the departing bus. Was there a "doorway?" that I was failing to see?

A hiss on the road behind me startled me out of my reverie, and I turned to see a bicyclist race past me on the steep downhill slope.

Too fast. He left it till too late to brake for the next hairpin, and the bike slid out from under him on the wet roadway. He went down hard on the pavement.

He lay still on the roadway. I jogged down the slope, calling out, "Are you hurt? Are you okay?"

No response.

I threw off my pack and knelt beside him. His eyes were closed. I didn't know much first-aid, but I reached out to touch his throat to see if there was a pulse.

As I did, his eyes flickered, then opened. After a moment, they focused on me. "Well, seems I've made a right fool of myself, haven't I?"

"You fell," I said, stating the obvious.

"So it appears." He moved each arm, then each leg, then rolled up to a sitting position. "Doesn't seem as though I've broken anything. Thank God I was wearing a helmet."

He pulled the helmet off. His hair was silver, and I guessed him at perhaps 50.

"You're the hiker I just passed, aren't you? Just before I took my tumble?"

"That was me."

"I was thinking how much sooner I'd be back in the village than you," he laughed. "The tortoise and the hare. Serves me right for being distracted. For being uncharitable, too."

He took my hand, and maneuvered himself to his feet. He had a nasty scrape on one knee, another on his elbow.

He hobbled over to his bike. That was not in as good shape: one wheel was twisted like a potato chip.

"So much for today's adventures, " he said, checking out the rest of the bike. Then he turned to me, "Care for a ride back to the village?"

"On that?" If he thought one person could ride it now, let alone two, then must have gotten a concussion.

He laughed. "Of course not." He reached into the pouch behind the bike's saddle and pulled out a cellular phone. "I'll just call us a taxi."

I felt a chill pass up my spine: The Becoming May be an Opening Door.

37

I OVERSLEPT ON MY FINAL MORNING. Subconsciously, I suppose, I didn't want to leave. But leave I had to, like it or not.

Alas, that first thing going wrong—sleeping too long—seemed to set off a chain of other things going wrong—just as back in the bad old days before I stumbled upon Brother Freddie and the Knowledge.

Breakfast, normally on the table as soon as I sat in the chair, was slow today. Then it seemed to take forever for the clerk to figure up my bill. The taxi was slow in coming, so finally I grabbed my bags and headed to the station on foot.

I was determined not to let the setbacks throw me into the kind of negative, self-defeating mindset they would have in the past. But it wasn't easy. The old mantras were lurking in the background, ready to take over again: Whatever *can* go wrong *will* go wrong, and, Once *one* thing goes wrong, *everything* else goes wrong.

I raced to the train station, and arrived just as the conductor blew his whistle. The brakes released with a sigh, and the little train eased forward.

I shouted "Wait! Wait!" but no one heard me. I grabbed my bags and ran after the train. If I missed the train, then I would miss my flight, and my ticket wasn't transferable. Use it or lose it.

How can this be? I had "selected" to have an easy, uneventful journey, arriving home on time with all my luggage. And yet, at each step in the journey, it was falling apart.

"I *am* going to make that train," I told myself, even as I stood on the platform watching it go. "I *am*. I *am*."

Then the train slowed and stopped.

I found it hard to believe what I was seeing. Was I experiencing a miracle?

I jumped off the platform and ran along the track, luggage dangling under my arms. The station master shouted to me to come back, but I ignored him and kept going.

Now I saw what had stopped the train: a flock of cows had just then decided to meander across the track. I made it to the last car and pounded on the door. Someone hit the button, and I climbed aboard just before the train lurched forward again.

"The Track We Select is the Track that Becomes," I thought as I settled into a seat. In this case it literally *was* a track—a *train* track.

That message came to mind: *The Becoming May be an Opening Door.*

The person I was when I arrived at the village would have stood up on the platform, watching the train leave, wallowing in the old self-pity, believing the world was out to frustrate me. And those negative expectations would have been fulfilled.

But now I recognized that the Becoming may be an opening door—that reality is not fixed, that I can choose to be more than just a passive victim of random events, that by my expectations I can be a "shaper" of the version of reality that I encounter.

Of course, the question hangs out there: Did my expectations somehow bring about the result? Did my determination somehow cause those cows to happen to select that moment to cross the tracks? I'll never know the answer.

But what I was, even then, already finding, was that it seemed to be a matter of *probabilities*. Those times when I made the effort to select the outcome I desired, and to hold that expectation firmly, unwaveringly in mind, I did seem to seem to tip the odds in my favor.

Brother Freddie: *What better scientist than yourself for experimenting in the reality around you?*

IT WAS A SHORT RIDE DOWN THE MOUNTAIN, and I used the time to renew my expectation of an easy and perfect trip home, with all my luggage arriving intact with me. Once one thing goes right, everything goes right, I assured myself.

The connection from the railway station to the airport went smoothly, and it was easy to hold that expectation of an easy and uneventful journey.

But then I got to the check-in counter, and found the airline had lost my reservation. I had locked in a window seat for the return flight. Now, it turned out, that spot had already been given to someone else, and all that were left were middle seats, jammed tightly between two strangers.

For an instant, I felt myself slipping into the anger and frustration that used to be normal response to situations. I wanted to tell the clerk how her airline couldn't seem to get anything right, how they had lost my luggage on the way over, and now they had given away the seat I'd reserved weeks ago.

"You have to fight for what you get in life," my father still says at least once each week, a message he's been sharing for as long as I can remember. "They try to stick it to little people like us when they're dishing out the good things in life. They'll usually get away with it, but if you fight, you can leave some blood on the floor . . . and it won't be only *your* blood."

I took a deep breath. I was going to fight. Chances were I'd still be stuck in the middle seat, but at least—

Then it was as if Brother Freddie were beside me, nudging me in the ribs. *Hold your positive expectation. Expect a perfect flight.*

The clerk punched some more commands into the computer, then frowned at what came up on the screen. "There was a problem with your luggage on the way over, yes?"

I nodded. "The plane was delayed with mechanical problems, then my bag was lost for a day."

She smiled. "Then I think we should do something to make up for that." She punched the keyboard again, then smiled when the new screen came up. "Now I have a window seat for you."

"Wonderful."

"And it is in Business Class. You should have a very nice flight there: the food is better, and the seats wider."

38

I FOUND MYSELF SEATED NEXT TO a businessman, and we got talking. By that point on the way home, I was beginning to think about what I would do for a job. It would be nice to say that my seat-mate offered me a position, but it didn't happen that way.

However, from the chance event of being upgraded to Business Class and seated next to him, I got something even better for the long term than a job offer. That contact, and the chance to listen in on his way of thinking, broadened my horizons and made me aware of a different way of working.

The Becoming May Be an Opening Door.

Years back, when I finished school, my family prodded me to go for something safe, something "with a secure future." (Little did we know then how insecure "secure jobs" would turn out to be.)

To play it safe, I took the first job that seemed to meet those criteria. The work didn't fit my talents or interests, but, as my father said so many times, "Work isn't *supposed* to be enjoyable, it's just what you do until you pick up the paycheck."

Since then, each of my jobs have been a progression from that same starting point. Because I wasn't particularly good at what I did, the promotions had been few over the years.

Worse, I had lost sight of the fact that there were other ways of earning a living, and that maybe I should try another kind of work.

It was—I can see now as I look back—another instance of the workings of The Track We Select is the Track that Becomes.

I had expected—hence "selected"—a career of difficulties, limitations, drudgery. And so that was what I experienced.

I had taken for granted that I was locked for life into this career track.

I had assumed that, since I had been inept in *this kind* of work that I'd be equally inept and unsuccessful in *every* kind of work—and again that expectation became a reality because I never even tried to make a change . . . until I lost my job and was forced to change.

ONCE I BEGAN TALKING TO MY COMPANION ON THE PLANE, I realized that I had let myself become trapped into a very narrow view of what I could do. I had developed the expectation that all I *could* do was what I *had* done—even though I hadn't done that very well.

In that conversation, I managed to draw back from looking at the *specific* things I did to get a look at myself in *context of the whole* operation.

Yes, I had been trapped for too long in dealing with details. But that time, I suddenly realized, had not all been wasted. I had been trapped in the details, but they were details from all across the operation.

Now I now realized that I'd gained unique, broad insight on how organizations really functioned, and what worked and what did not.

With a little special training, I could do something like what my seat-mate did—and get paid far more than I had ever dreamed of.

Or I could take my experience and jump up several steps on the organizational ladder, because I had both the specific how-to skill with the details, plus a broad perspective backed up by experience.

In short, my options were far wider than I had ever realized. I had the skills and the experience. All I needed were the breaks, especially someone to recognize that I had what it takes to jump upward.

I had never gotten the breaks in the past . . . but then I had never *expected* to get the breaks.

Now I did. Now I knew that what I expected—specifically, what I *chose* to expect—*would* be what became.

39

DAYS PASSED BEFORE JACKIE, as overwhelmed as ever by work, could find the time to talk about (to use Jackie's term) "our situation."

When we did get together, it was clear from the start that there would be no marriage, not now, not ever.

The decision was mutual, though I had some trouble accepting it. It's hard to let go of something that seems "safe," when you don't yet know if there is ever going to be anything as good coming along. But it must be done, regardless, if you're ever going to be able to move on to something even better.

Besides, it was evident by now that Jackie and I had moved in very different ways. Jackie seemed to reflect the person I used to be. Now I was very glad that I had taken steps to move away from that negative, fear-driven person, so lacking in confidence in myself and the potential of the universe.

But Jackie's perception was very different. Now I had become "flaky," "irresponsible," "a dreamer."

"The thing you should do is buckle down, recognize your limitations, recognize the fact that you're not getting any younger, and try to find a job like the one you had, one you're sure you can handle."

But I had no desire to go back to being the limited, anxiety-ridden, unhappy person I had been—and that made Jackie "concerned and worried" about me.

40

ONE MAJOR CAUSE OF CONTENTION WAS the house we had bought just before I lost my job.

With the wedding cancelled, and our friendship close to ended, it was evident that Jackie and I would never live in the house.

Jackie was panicky, and wanted to find a buyer to take it over from us at any cost. "I don't like losing hard-earned money any more than you do, but at least we should cut our losses as fast as we can."

If I were as I had been a month earlier, I'd probably have agreed. Back then, we lived by the same world-view: Don't take risks. Things can only get worse. Whatever *can* go wrong will go wrong.

But I'd been living with the Knowledge for long enough now that I was opposed to settling for a sure, predictable loss. If we *expected* a loss, and were willing to settle for a loss, then we'd *get* a loss, no question of that. The track we join is the track that becomes.

But there was no guarantee that the loss would stay within the limits we set.

On the other hand, if we selected the Reality Track in which the perfect outcome resulted, then I was convinced we'd not only escape without losing money, but might even make some.

BUT JACKIE DIDN'T WANT TO HEAR THAT.

"We need to be realistic. The fact is that this is not a good time of year to be selling a house. People are going to see that we bought, then immediately wanted to sell it, and they'll figure that the house is flawed. We're going to lose money, beyond any doubt. The sooner we bite the bullet and do it, the better."

"But those are all negative expectations," I tried to say.

"They're not *expectations*, they're *realities*."

"What we expect is what becomes, so—"

"There you go again with that spooky mumbo-jumbo. If I hear one more time about selecting a positive Reality Track, I'll—well, I'll be sick. It's time to get out of dreamland and face reality."

"Why is your view of reality so consistently negative and limiting? " I said, the words slipping out.

"Because, whether you like it or not, *that* is the way the world *is!* I'm simply realistic. What we need to do is list the house with a broker tomorrow and get things moving, fast. Every week that we're stuck with it costs money for the mortgage and insurance. Meanwhile, real estate prices will probably drop even further."

"Another way of looking at it is that every month we hold the house gives us 30 more days for the perfect buyer to come along at the perfect price."

"No buyers are going to pop up, you need to face that fact. It's going to take a very aggressive broker who really knows how to market a flawed house."

Brother Freddie, I realized then, had failed to tell me what happens when one partner's expectations are positive and the other's are solidly negative. Whose expectations prevail?

"If we list it with a broker, and if we sell it at the exact price we bought it, then that—"

"That's totally unrealistic. There is no possibility of our ever selling it for the price we paid. We'll be lucky if we get 80% of that."

"But even if we did manage to sell it at that price through a broker, then we'd immediately lose money because of the broker's commission."

"There's no chance of our selling it on our own, so face facts: We need a professional, a broker, to handle it for us."

Had I really been like that, I marveled, so solidly locked into the negative? No wonder the only luck I ever had was *bad* luck. That's what I was expecting, and what turned up.

"How do we know there's no chance unless we try?"

"I know because I live in the real world."

I figured that was probably not the best time to tell about Brother Freddie's ideas on how the real, solid table is really 99.99% empty space.

I HAD PUT UP MORE THAN HALF OF THE MONEY for the deposit, so Jackie reluctantly agreed to give me a month to try to sell it on my own.

So that was how I spent my next four weekends, sitting for the open houses we advertised. It wasn't bad. I actually enjoyed it. It gave me time to catch up the diary from my trip, and the memories were fresh enough that I was able to capture most of what Brother Freddie said.

That diary would come in handy—but that's a story for later.

The time wasn't all solitary. I met a lot of interesting people, one of whom would play an important role in my life later. And I learned a lot about how to sell and relate to people in a way that I had never learned in all my years of work before.

I'd never tried selling in the past because, frankly, I didn't have the confidence. I was afraid that people would say no because they didn't like me, or didn't trust me.

But now I found that selling wasn't at all like that. The experience taught me that selling is really about finding ways of helping people fill their needs, and I learned how to listen and ask questions so I could find what those needs were. Once I knew what they needed, then I could help them understand the ways in which the house met those needs.

The Becoming May be an Opening Door.

41

BUT THE FINAL DAY OF THE FINAL WEEKEND came and went, and we still didn't have a buyer. A few people had come close to making an offer, and one couple even came back for a second and then a third look, before buying another place.

I was surprised and discouraged when I closed up that final afternoon.

Discouraged because it meant we'd be signing with the agent we'd talked to, another "realist" like Jackie, who had begun by telling us that now we were in the low-season, and the only chance we'd have of selling would be to cut the price. Then of course there would be his commission coming off the top of whatever we did get.

As I said, I was surprised that we hadn't found a buyer. Hadn't I been confident enough in my expectation of finding a perfect buyer? Had I failed to make clear that I had selected going down the Reality Track that had a "Sold" sign waiting at the end?

Or had Jackie's persisting fears and negative expectations drowned out mine?

I WAS TIRED AND HUNGRY WHEN I CLOSED UP after my final afternoon of sitting the house, and didn't feel like grocery-shopping and then cooking. It was tempting to stop in a restaurant and let somebody else do the work.

"But restaurants are expensive," I heard the little voice inside my head saying. "You're going to take a big loss on the house. You don't have a job in sight. You'd better not squander money on restaurant food."

A couple of months ago I would have listened to that voice—the voice of diminishing expectations.

But not now. Now there was another voice, another message. Now I understood. I had the freedom to join the track I preferred.

IT WAS JUST A NEIGHBORHOOD CAFÉ, normally almost empty on a late Sunday afternoon. I almost backed out when I saw the crowd, but Mama Lucia, the owner, spotted me and led me to a table before I could slip away. I was tired and down, and really didn't want to share a table with strangers.

But it turned out to be just one more instance of The Becoming Being an Opening Door. In a way I would soon grasp, that string of chance events opened up possibilities I could never have foreseen.

It was a busy evening, service was slow, and I got talking with the couple whose table I was sharing. It turned out they were visiting our town because the company they worked for was opening a facility here—a bit of news that yet hadn't made it into the local media.

That, I suddenly realized, meant two things.

First, the local real estate market was about to boom, with new people arriving and needing places to live.

Second, the universe, in its strange ways, had put me at the table with one of those possible buyers. They were interested in my house, and interested in moving quickly. They drove over with me to look at it after dinner, then came back in the morning, and signed the contract to buy before lunch-time.

"I'M SHOCKED, ABSOLUTELY AMAZED," Jackie said upon hearing the news. "I never expected we'd find a buyer at all, let alone one willing to pay the asking price."

"I expected we would. Not just expected, but *Expected*, capital E, as in The Track we Expect is the Track that Becomes."

"There you go, on that nonsense again! We were *lucky*, just very lucky, nothing more than that."

"It was—"

"It went too easily. That concerns me, when things go too well. I expect that something will come up at the last minute and we'll be worse off than before we started."

Don't expect that, don't even think it!, I wanted to say. But I held back, because if I had that really would have fired up Jackie's furnace of negative expectations.

IT WAS, ALAS, THE TRACK JACKIE EXPECTED that turned out to be the track that came true.

A week before the closing was to take place, I got a call from the buyers. Circumstances had changed, and they were being transferred to a different branch, not here. "Which means, sadly, that we won't be able to buy your house, after all."

I held the phone, not knowing what to say. *"But we have a contract! You can't just walk away!"* the old me would have said, turning it into a battle of wills.

Then I thought of Brother Freddie reaching up to point to the words carved on the wall as he translated for me: *"There's always a gate. Look for the gate."*

Instead of screaming, My lawyer will be calling your lawyer!, I asked, "Is your company still planning to set up the facility here in town?"

Hold the expectation, I told myself. *Expect that the sale will still go through.*

"That's still on schedule. If you like, I can post a picture of the house here on the company bulletin board."

42

"I *KNEW* IT! I JUST *KNEW* IT! DIDN'T I *TELL* YOU SOMETHING WOULD GO WRONG!" Jackie said, sounding almost pleased at the turn in events.

Next morning, as promised, Jackie called to tell me I needed to report to a realtor's office after work to sign the papers. "Of course, since you're still out of work, you can take that to mean five o'clock."

As things turned out, I never showed up to sign those papers.

Just after noon I got a call from somebody who had seen that posting on the company bulletin board; and I met them at the house an hour later. They gave me a check on the spot to bind the agreement.

IT'S STRANGE HOW THINGS WORK OUT. Not only did we manage to sell the house, and even make a little profit, but beyond that the buyer put me in touch with the person doing the hiring for the new facility here.

But it wasn't that neat.

That company didn't need anybody with my particular skills. Which was not really disappointing, as I didn't really want to use those skills any more.

But what came out of that meeting was the confirmation that I had skills beyond those I thought I had. I had been looking too narrowly at myself and what I could do, and the person who interviewed me was kind enough to point that out.

Yes, I had mastered the details of my old job, but now I recognized that I had learned a lot more than just that.

One thing led to another—actually, one introduction led to another introduction, and then to a third. Before long, I found myself in a new city, in a new job, earning a lot more than I ever would had I stayed safely where I had been.

ONCE ONE THING GOES RIGHT, EVERYTHING GOES RIGHT—that's my newest Rule of Life.

I enjoyed the new life and the new work. I enjoyed having the extra money to spend, and I spent a good bit of it at the start upgrading my wardrobe so I began to feel even better about myself. No longer was I wearing whatever I found on sale, and no longer did I wear those things until they were "tired."

Now I was expecting that prosperity was the norm. No more did I see good things as a warning of hard times to come.

I met new people and made new friends—and, not really surprising, most of those new friends were the kind of upbeat, cheerful people who were enjoyable to be around.

One of those new friends was Terry.

VI   THE BECOMING MAY BE AN OPENING DOOR

❑   Be patient: your 'expectation' may not be fulfilled immediately . . . or even soon.

❑   Be flexible: it may not come in precisely the form you anticipated.

❑   Be creative: sometimes you may need to examine how what appears is, in perhaps an unexpected form, the ideal fulfillment of your expectation.

❑   Recognize that a setback may be a signpost, directing you to look for a better way or an even better goal.

❑   Look for the doorway. It may not be obvious, but, once found, it may lead to a better way of achieving your goal.

❑   Above all, hold confidence in your selection. *Expect* it, don't just hope for it.

❑   If you select properly, you set the probabilities in your favor. You increase the probability that things will work out the way you want, or perhaps even better—provided you are open to unanticipated ways.

VII

BECAUSE THE INFINITE IS INFINITE, IT CANNOT BE USED UP

43

"PRACTICE! IT TAKES PRACTICE," Brother Freddie had said as I was leaving. "Don't be reluctant to use your power. It's not something you risk using up. On the contrary, it's like a skill, or like a muscle. It strengthens with practice."

I'd been using the power more and more in those first weeks home as I slowly began realizing that there was potential for improvement within situations that I'd previously have given up as unfortunate but totally unavoidable..

Now I understood that I was *not* a victim of circumstances, and recognized that many of these *were* within my span of control—not my *direct* control, of course, but *indirectly*, by my expectations. I could control my thoughts, and hence my expectations . . . and my expectations played a key role in shaping the events that came to be.

I *did* have a choice. I could accept things as they were, or I could choose to expect something better—and, astonishingly often, something better did indeed emerge.

Not always, but way more than mere chance.

Back in the bad old days, I'd go to the health club on Saturdays, "knowing" that all the machines I wanted would already be in use . . . and inevitably I'd be right. Now I go on Saturdays confidently expecting that the machines I want will be open when I'm ready for them. Maybe I should keep a log (hard to do in exercise garb!), but my guess is that at least nine times out of ten the machine I want is ready when I am.

Mel, a friend from years back, had an incredible knack for driving through town and, no matter how crowded it was, finding an open parking slot right where he wanted it. "How can one person be so lucky!" I used to marvel. "It's not luck," he'd respond, "it's a kind of knowing that a spot will open up for me."

I'd written that off as nonsense at the time, but now I was beginning to understand. Even better, now I was finding that I was as skilled as Mel in finding a spot when I need it. He called it "knowing," I call it "Expecting"—with a capital E.

"A long weekend? Then that means rain, for sure." That was my old mindset, and—I have to tell you, I was a better predictor than any TV weather-guy. Never again will I even *think* thoughts, like "A day off means rain," or "My toast always falls jelly-side down," or, "Just my luck, there won't be any tickets left when I finally get up to the counter."

BUT THERE WAS STILL THAT NAGGING THOUGHT: Was I using up all my share of good fortune on small things like parking spaces and exercise machines?

I phoned Brother Freddie with that question. Not only had he acquired a cell-phone in the weeks since I left the monastery, but the phone had a built-in camera. It was good to see his face again.

"Ah, my friend," he responded, "tell me: why do you think the world is so limited?"

"For one thing, there are only so many parking places in a town—that is a limitation."

"True, but isn't it a matter of timing? Not every space is used every minute, so is it not reasonable to expect that you will arrive at the juncture point when that space chances to be free?"

I had an image of some vast computer trying to schedule parking spaces across the various permutations of potential realities. "But how can anybody, any computer, schedule that?"

"Who needs to schedule? Your expectation puts you into a version of the universe in which the parking space is open. Or the reverse, if your expectations incline that way."

I told him about my health club and my experience with the exercise machines that never used to be free, and now always seemed to be waiting just for me.

He seemed to understand . . . even though I doubt he'd ever seen a mirrored exercise gym filled with an array of treadmills and bikes and weight machines populated by a platoon of sweaty people puffing away a week of inactivity and big lunches.

"The universe is infinite," he replied.

"The universe may be infinite, but my health club is finite. There are only so many machines."

"Do you know what infinite means?

"Sure, unlimited."

"How many numbers are there between 1 and 3?"

I hesitated. Another trick question? "Well, there's the number 2, smack-dab in between 1 and 3."

"Ah, very good. You deserve an A. But how many numbers are there between 1 and 2?"

"None?" I said, figuring he had a trick up the sleeve of his monk's robe.

"Really? Aren't you forgetting 1.5, smack-dab, as you say, between 1 and 2?"

"I didn't realize you were including decimals."

"How many numbers between 1.4 and 1.5?"

"If you look at it that way, then it depends on how far you want to carry it. There's 1.4.1, 1.4.2—"

"You make my point. How far could you carry it, breaking down the distance between one number and the next? Think about it. You'll see that there are an *infinite* number of numbers, if you want to carry it to as many decimals as you can imagine. That's a practical example of infinity."

"Hmm," was all I could say.

"Now tell me, what's the largest number you can think of?"

"How long do you have to listen while I say it?"

"As long as it takes. And then I'll ask you to tell me the next number beyond that. And then the next—more examples of real-world infinity. No matter how large the number is, there is always one larger . . . and another larger than that."

"Once again, I'm not sure where you're heading with this."

"You asked me how it was that you could possibly hope to always find a space on the machine you wanted when you wanted it. I suggested that perhaps the answer is that by your expectations you step into the version of the universe where that space is free, when you want it."

"But there's only one version of my health club."

"Is there? Some would suggest that there are an infinity of health clubs, identical to yours, waiting to be populated at any moment. In some, the machines are all taken, while in others, the machine you want is available."

HE SET HIS CAMERA-PHONE ON A TABLE so I could see him as he and walked over to the chapel wall and pointed as before to one of the inscriptions carved into the stone wall, translating for me as his fingers traced he words:

BECAUSE THE INFINITE IS INFINITE,

IT CANNOT BE USED UP.

VII   BECAUSE THE INFINITE *IS* INFINITE, IT CANNOT BE USED UP

❏   Is there a risk of using up all your share of "good fortune" by choosing to join small things like available parking spaces and exercise machines?

❏   Some who work in the field of quantum physics suggest that there are an infinite number of nearly identical universes, waiting to be populated. They use the term "multiverses."

❏   Your expectation puts you into a version of the multiverse in which the parking space is open. Or the reverse, if your expectations incline that way.

❏   So there is no need to be reluctant to use your power. It's not something you risk using up. On the contrary, it's like a skill, or like a muscle. It strengthens with practice.

VIII

ALL
IS THE GREAT
EXPECTATION
OF THE ONE

44

A COUPLE OF YEARS PASSED, and it seemed that my life evolved for the better in every way. I thrived at work now that I was finally in the right kind of job and expecting to succeed and prosper.

Now I was good at what I did. Or was it that I was finally doing the kind of work I did well?

I had made the effort to "expect" the perfect job, and to have my efforts appreciated. Within the first year, I found myself promoted two levels.

Was it—to use my old phrase—"mere coincidence" that the people in those jobs happened to move on, making room for me to move up?

Or was it the working out of events in a framework that I had set up by my expectations?

Certainly there were not, as Brother Freddie had once joked with me, "the sounding of trumpets or the crashing of thunder" to announce that something extraordinary had happened. The changes were, as he had warned me they would be, subtle, often what seemed to be random coincidences.

But it was not only on the job that my life moved for the better.

As I mentioned, I met Terry, and we clicked from the start.

When we married, it seemed only right to visit Brother Freddie and share with him our good news.

Whatever can go right will go right, and once one thing went right everything went right. We had an easy flight, our luggage arrived with us, and we caught the express train up to the village. A room was waiting for us, even nicer than the one that had finally turned up on my first visit.

Terry found the little village charming. "It's just what I'd envisioned . . . or even better."

But then after dinner the rain rolled in, and the weather report predicted two days of heavy spring rains.

That was a blow. We had rain-gear and boots with us, so the weather wouldn't stop us, but I'd been looking forward to bringing Terry up that trail for the first time, with its spectacular views of the village below and the snow-capped mountains above.

Then I bounced back from the disappointment, and set about "expecting" good weather for morning.

WHAT I EXPECTED, BECAME. The wind picked up overnight, and by morning the rain and clouds had blown away, and it was one of those crystal-clear days you only get in the mountains, a great day to be alive.

The chapel was just as I remembered it, still tucked away in the overhang of the tall old pine trees.

We entered, and I brought Terry over to see the inscriptions carved into the wall. We had talked about the messages almost from the day we met, so the wall came as no surprise.

"It's hard to believe I'm finally here," Terry said.

"It's hard to believe I'm finally back," I replied, louder than necessary because I was expecting Brother Freddie to materialize from the shadows at any moment.

But he didn't. Finally I called out his name. Still he didn't appear.

I led the way out of the chapel and along the arched walkway—which I had since learned was termed a "cloister." I knocked at the door of the main building. No reply. I didn't want to intrude, so we walked the grounds. I figured Brother Freddie might be in his garden. But he wasn't, and the garden didn't seem to have been planted yet.

Now I was getting concerned.

We headed back to the monastery. I knocked. No reply. I pushed against the heavy old wooden door, and it swung open.

But now there were no aromas of spicy soup brewing, or apples baking. The building seemed cold and empty.

"Hello," I called out, fear growing. "Brother Freddie, are you there?"

We went on to the library. I pushed the door open. The room was bare. His television and video recorder were gone, and the books had been taken from the shelves. The chairs where we had sat for those long afternoons were gone.

The only thing left in the room was the old wooden table. The one he'd pointed to when he'd asked me, "Is this table real?," then explained why I might see it as solid, but a physicist would not see a solid table. "To a physicist, the table you see as solid and real is mostly empty space with a few bits of what we think of matter."

Tears filled my eyes now, because I knew I wouldn't be seeing Brother Freddie again, and I went over and knocked on the wood as on that first day, and the knock echoed in the empty room.

THAT WAS WHEN I NOTICED THE BROWN ENVELOPE on the table. I was stunned to see my name written on the front.

By then Terry understood, too, that there would be no chance to meet Brother Freddie, and we hugged before I open it.

When we met, you asked me if there were other monks here. I said I was the only one now, but that I expected that a new Keeper of the Knowledge would come when the time was right.

Times have changed in the years since I arrived here and became the Keeper. That was long before there were digital video and scanning electron microscopes to explore the reality beneath the reality, and before videotapes to record what was there, and before computers and cellular phones and faxes and all the new ways that exist today to communicate knowledge . . . Particularly what you and I know as "The Knowledge."

Whether for better or worse I don't know, but people have changed, too, and it seems there will not be a monk coming to be the new Keeper of the Knowledge. Perhaps that is best.

Perhaps it is time to change from waiting for people to COME TO the Knowledge and instead use the new communications to BRING the Knowledge TO the people who are not able to come here.

I have taken the liberty to put your name on the small blank book you will find in the drawer of the table, and to write the first sentence in the hope that you will finish the story in the way that you think best conveys the Knowledge for people today.

With love and prayer,
Brother Freddie

I OPENED THE DRAWER , TURNED TO THE FIRST PAGE OF THE SMALL BOOK, and read what I found there: "My foot slipped on the wet rock, and I felt the ankle twist and snap."

It was a small book covered in leather like the books that had filled the shelves when Brother Freddie was here.

IN THE MONASTERY GRAVEYARD, now nearly overgrown with trees and shrubs, we found the stones lined up in rows, small, simple gravestones, each marked with the name of a monk, and the years he had lived.

Brother Freddie's stone had not yet collected moss.

FREDERICUS NONANUS

I remembered enough Latin to know it meant that my friend Brother Freddie was the ninth monk in this monastery over the years to bear the name Frederick. I wondered if he was the first with the sense of humor to call himself Brother Freddie.

We collected some wild flowers and formed them into a bouquet and brought them to the grave. We knelt and prayed for the kindly old man who had given us so much.

And then I said aloud, "Of course, Brother Freddie, I'll finish the book. You were the last *Keeper* of the Knowledge. Now I'll do my best to be the first *Spreader* of the Knowledge. I only hope I'm up to the responsibility."

Then it seemed as if I heard someone whisper in my ear, "Don't just *hope*. Select the Reality Track in which it happens. What we expect, becomes. *Expect* that you will be."

I   REALITY IS NOT AS IT SEEMS.

Given that neither the "things" around me, such as rocks and chairs and cars and even my body, are not really solid, but rather wispy things that are 99.99% empty space, what does that tell me about the issues and concerns with which I am involved in my daily life?

II   ALL POTENTIAL REALITIES ALREADY EXIST.

Given also that modern science indicates that all potential versions of reality already exist in a latent form, waiting for the intervention of human consciousness to bring one version to the actuality we experience, then what might that mean for me on the practical level of everyday life?

III   THE TRACK WE JOIN IS THE TRACK THAT BECOMES.

Can I accept—as a deep belief, and not just with words or wishes—that I have the power or capability to step across and join an alternate track in reality?

How can I act in a practical way in focusing and disciplining my mind and thoughts to accomplish that act of joining another version among the infinity of versions that already exist?

**IV   WHAT MAY SEEM TO BE UNUSUAL
COINCIDENCES ARE MERELY NORMAL
HAPPENINGS IN A DIFFERENT REALITY TRACK.**

When I encounter a strange, seemingly coincidental, turn of events, do I look back at my own expectations, as well as what I can discern were the actual expectations of others, and try to determine what mindsets or expectations may have played a role in manifesting this unexpected synchronicity?

**V   THE PRESENT TRACK EVIDENCES
PAST EXPECTATIONS.**

Do I look at the situations in which I find myself, and ask, Given the fact that I have arrived at this present situation, what must have been the expectations that placed me there?

Am I inadvertently joining a version of reality that I will later regret? If so, what can I change?

Have I perhaps been associating with people whose wrong or limiting expectations have drawn me into reality tracks different than I would have chosen for myself?

VI   THE BECOMING MAY BE AN OPENING DOOR.

How open am I to unexpected turns of events? Am I more inclined to view them as upsetting, or as opportunities that allow, or even prod, me to move in new ways and new directions?

How open am I to apparent setbacks as signposts to unexpected possibilities?

Do I stay alert and open to the opportunities offered by unexpected doorways—even those that at first seem to signal problems or disappointments?

VII   BECAUSE THE INFINITE *IS* INFINITE, IT CANNOT BE USED UP.

Have I ever been afraid of "using up" my reservoir of good fortune?

VIII   ALL IS THE GREAT EXPECTATION OF THE ONE.

Do I accept the responsibility that flows from the insight that I am not just a bystander or observer in this world we all jointly experience, but rather a participant and co-creator?

Have you seen the on-line flash movies that provide background on

Joining Miracles:
Navigating the Seas of Latent Possibility

and the related spiritual thriller,

The Grail Conspiracies

ISBN-10: 0-9768406-0-X
ISBN-13: 978-0976840602

See those videos at **www.JoiningMiracles.com**
and at **www.TheGrailConspiracies.com**

About the author

Michael McGaulley, author of *Joining Miracles: Navigating the Seas of Latent Possibility* and the related *The Grail Conspiracies*, a spiritual thriller, is a lawyer and management consultant.

These books bring together his interest in the intersection of the spiritual and metaphysical with the possibilities raised by the new physics' discoveries that the world is very different than we assume.

Printed in the United States
81712LV00007B/226-246